HAVE GUITAR
WILL TRAVEL

HAVE GUITAR
WILL TRAVEL

by
Neil Smith

CARNMOR PRINT

Printed by Carnmor Print
95/97, London Road, PRESTON, Lancs. PR1 4BA
Tel: 01772 555615

PRELUDE

When you next see a well-travelled musician on stage or television, just for a moment, pause and try to imagine the lifestyle of that person. Forget your safe, regular job based near home and family. Many musicians travel over 100,000 miles in a year these days and a few will circuit the globe in a month, living purely by using their talented fingers, from plane to hotel, to the hall and back and so on for years. What is it really like for such a player, a modern-day Troubadour? HAVE GUITAR, WILL TRAVEL is Neil Smith's travelogue, stringing together famous names like Elizabeth Taylor, Anna Ford and Adolf Hitler along with trips to the Grand Canyon, the castle of Attila the Hun, and great halls of the world. Not only can we meet the rich and famous in these pages but also the downright evil and deadly out there who prey on the innocent voyager.

Neil traces his early musical roots through The Sixties describing a whole host of characters from the Show Business facade, combining factual and realistic observation with humour and nostalgia. We voyage with him across state-lines, on through difficult tours and many dangerous journeys into the unknown as he attempts to make his mark in the World of Music. En route, he describes everything of interest: the ruined castle of the dreaded Attila, scourge of the Romans, an evening spent playing for Elizabeth Taylor and an attack after midnight by a crazed-killer. Read how his tutor describes her own school days to Neil....when she sat next to Adolf Hitler for a year in class! And we meet some war-heroes, one of whom was captured by the famous Desert Fox (Rommel) and another who fought against Rommel's mentor in the towering inferno of the Battle of Kursk in Russia.

This is not simply another biography nor is it exclusively for musicians. In part, it traces a very individual path through today's world and brings to life scenes which are truly amazing and unrepeatable. Transporting the reader to far-flung destinations, Neil gives colour and texture to his stories allowing us to share the moment with him and make each moment a part of our own life-experience. An absolute must for anyone involved or interested in the musical profession, here we have a book that is entertaining, witty, factual and at times, deadly serious to the point of chilling accuracy. A sure-fire collection of true stories guaranteed to remain in the memory for a long time.

MY THANKS TO....

Many people have obviously contributed to this volume but, without certain friends, it would not have appeared in print. I first want to thank Doreen and Harry Knipe from Cumbria for their continuing support in all of my work and their direct support for this book. Also Jane Marsh, Christine Denmead and my partner Elaine for the difficulties they faced trying to proofread this collection, also to those who supplied the photos from around the world. For the record, some events here could not be captured on film; the danger was real, the event so fast, the security so tight that no bystander could have possibly aimed and took a posed shot. The loss is both mine and yours.

I may also say here that as I read this text again, it occurred to me that I have led a charmed life: in effect (as the reader will see) I could have easily been killed on several occasions. I hope the result is both interesting and entertaining.

Neil Smith

Published by Neil Smith
© Neil Smith
THE GALLERY
177 LEE LANE
HORWICH
GTR. MANCHESTER
BL6 7JD
ENGLAND
Website: www.guitaristuk.com
Printed 2001
ISBN 0-9541430-0-0

JACKET PHOTO
Antony Good

CONTENTS

SEE ROME, SEE CLEOPATRA....AND LIVE!

DARK, SATANIC MILLS....

I'VE GOT RHYTHM, I'VE GOT MUSIC....

SWINGING SIXTIES....

WAR AND PEACE....

HAVE YOU ANYTHING TO DECLARE?

TRAINS, BOATS, PLANES....AND TANKS?

PLAY IT AGAIN, SAM....

TALES OF THE UNEXPECTED....

SEE ROME,
SEE CLEOPATRA....AND LIVE!

My family were not voyagers. My parents were the kind of couple who went everywhere together, they were lovely people and treated me well always. I guess that I was lucky having them close for a long time. Sadly, after my father died at the height of my career, it was not long before my mother killed herself....to be with him. Going way back in time, long before that terrible day, my father had been in the RAF out East and this had knocked out of him any desire to travel and consequently, my mother could see no point in moving around much. Conversely, I did want to travel, to go places and see everything and, with this in mind, I yearned to see the world, big mountains, valleys, oceans, deserts and I wanted to see it all, now, today!

Growing up in a small northern town like Horwich has many advantages and only my music pulled me away from these roots...and so my life was changed. The stereotype of Joe Lampton comes to mind in the black-and-white movies, a guy angry with the slow pace of life, angry with the limits set by other people and determined to change it all, even if it means moving heaven and earth. Often in the past, men and women went away and changed their name and appearance to start afresh. One such person was the daredevil fighter, Wild Bill Hickock and my first trip to the USA coincided with the 100th anniversary of his death; many papers reprinted the news from contemporary accounts....of how he was born and raised in Sheffield, England, and how he changed his name from Hitchcock because the Indians could not say 'Hitch' and of how he was shot in the back of the head in a saloon. There was a man who decided that 'normal' life was not for him. He left one of the northern cities as a steel-worker opting for a new life, thousands of miles from home, recalling his old life after much success out there, in the big world. Go West, Young Man, they used to say.

One Monday night, I wandered into my local pub and surveyed the usual scene. Why does Monday exist? As I pondered this earth-shaking theory, I heard some pals chatting earnestly about a planned trip to Rome on the next Friday. As I listened, it became clear that I should also join in this adventure and so, next day I bought sunglasses, shorts and a passport. The plan involved crossing The Alps in John's old Ford Zodiac, a couple of thousand miles or more with diversions. Friday night came and we eagerly filled the car with luggage, clipped my guitar on top and put a case of Heinz beans into the boot to keep us going on the trek. Overnight, we made Dover and got so drunk crossing The Channel that we had to sleep it off. We moved off from Oostende and the cities began to roll beneath our wheels....Gent, Bruxelles, Namur, Luxembourg, Saarbrucken, into the night we sped onwards and I took over the driving around 11pm. Heading fast at

100mph for Strasbourg, the instrument glow was my only company as everyone went off to sleep. John had suggested this high speed to make up lost time on the ferry. Suddenly, the car began to glide slightly sideways; I corrected this but there was a bump at the rear, enough to wake everyone in the car. John woke up and saw me turning the wheel from side to side; lights flashed behind me as other drivers warned us that a tyre had disintegrated! John held the wheel with me as I slowed down, the car becoming even more difficult to handle as the speed dropped and then....we were at the roadside; safe. Changing the wheel, we moved on, slower this time towards Basel and spent a super afternoon, drinking wine, eating cheese and fresh bread, playing guitar by a railtrack as the bees buzzed around our little party. By nightfall, we stopped by a lake....Lucerne in the moonlight. I cannot today listen to the Moonlight Sonata without seeing in my mind the little fire with a few cans of beans perched around the edge, a fond memory from the past, wild times.

By late evening, we had made Altdorf, the home of William Tell and beyond there, we halted at a tavern: out came the guitar and soon the whole place was in uproar. A rather wealthy gent asked us all back to his place: swimming pool, patio, wine, food....how could we refuse? Another wild night as the moonlight danced on the pool water. Beyond the magnificent Alps and the Gotthard, we ground along the Autostrada towards our goal, Rome, the Eternal City, and, by the following evening, we were entering the outskirts. I was dying of thirst, parched and baked by the sun on the long road: no wonder they call it Autostrada del Sol. Hot and dusty, we pulled up near a cafe/bar and a very beautiful woman stepped forwards to the car door and held the handle....I asked her for a place to buy ice-cream and she frowned. We got out the phrase book and told her.... "Sorbetto ....Glaciale....Gelato! She frowned again and shrugged her shoulders and said....OK! Only then did John realize what was going on; she was a street girl and thought that perhaps we had some weird fantasy with ice-cream in mind!

Rome was fantastic then, noisy and rather polluted but the whole place had a distinct 'buzz' about it all. We found a rather seedy set of rooms in the centre of the city: seedy enough to have mouse-traps all around the room. Walking around in the dark was like being in a war-zone! Our main hang-out was The Little Bar, an old, rather run-down place, with great atmosphere and, on occasion a visit from the famous. The guitarist there was Santino, character 'etched' deep into the lines on his face. He had been everywhere and, together, we made an odd couple as we toured the bars, never leaving until early light. One evening, we sat chatting near to the famous Trevi Fountain. I passed my guitar over to Santino and walked over to the fountain itself, sitting on the side, I gazed down into the shimmering water to see the coins at the bottom. Without any warning, John ran up behind me and pushed me in, head-first! I hit the coins with my feet and swam up to surface as hundreds of cameras flashed from near and far....coach-parties of people halted and took pictures of me as I struggled out, soaking wet. As I stood there, dripping onto the Piazza, two men from the Polizia came up and grabbed my arms tightly....I was under arrest! Technically, it is illegal to bathe in the fountain and so, I faced a possible night in jail! Things became more serious as a captain walked up and put his hand on my shoulder; he rasped out in very quick Italian a request for some form of ID....I produced my dripping, stuck-together passport and he opened it very carefully. On glancing inside he turned back to me....

"Ah....Americano? Stupido, stupido....Andare! Andare!"

The good fun seemed over; not quite. The night was young and I needed to dry off. I sat with Santino, watching John strolling around the Piazza, drinking, laughing, blissfully unaware of my plan. I waited and waited; 1am then 2am....nothing, he did not go near the water. Suddenly, he was sitting there, right on the edge as I had been! I ran as fast as possible and barged into him knocking him head-over-heels into the fountain! The Polizia by this time had realized that they were up against mad English and had retired to a safe distance.

During the weeks we stayed there, I became reasonably fluent when ordering food and drink and often wandered off alone, even at night. In the bar one evening, I sat along with Santino; everyone else was lying in bed too drunk or had wandered off to other bars. We played some very popular songs and applause filtered through from the side room now and again, the whole atmosphere was idyllic, perfect for a romance and Santino pointed out at the shimmering stars in the blue-velvet sky....

"Non possible England?"

No, I agreed, this was not possible in England anywhere, anytime. A man in a naval uniform came up to us; could we play The Spanish Romance? This melody is known around the world of course so this was not a problem. The man turned and pointed across to a dark corner of the room....

"Please play it for Miss Taylor."

Elizabeth Taylor was there, alongside Richard Burton. They were in town working on the film Cleopatra and had a yacht moored on the Tiber and this guy was obviously the skipper of their yacht! We played and they applauded as the candles flickered away at the table. Real-life film stars, I thought, sat listening to two crazy guitarists on one of the most blissful nights ever. Next day, I wandered out alone again on the Via Veneto, looking into the various shops and bars where the rich sat 'al-fresco'. Soon, I heard car horns sounding and a few whistles up ahead. The reason for the noise became obvious; sat at a table drinking coffee alone was Sophia Loren. She seemed quite undisturbed by all the fuss and looked incredible as I stared across the void between us. Briefly, she looked up and smiled at me as I watched, then went back to reading a magazine.

On one day, we decided to go to Naples; the car soon put a halt to that idea. As we motored through the avenues, people seemed to be shouting and pointing at the car front....

"Acqua, Acqua, ACQUA!!! ACQUA!!!!"

the cry went on and on as we drove on and on. Right in the middle of a crossroads, the car exploded, steam everywhere and a traffic-policeman walked over shouting and waving like crazy! We pushed the car off-road and left it for ages on yellow lines and on our return, vast numbers of tickets covered the windscreen....one of them was of more interest than the rest:

'You have parked illegally in our City. We understand that you are a foreigner and no action will be taken against you for this offence. We wish you a pleasant stay in Rome; please do not park in this way again.'

What nice, civilised people....imagine parking like this in England! What would be the penalty for three days on double-lines? A colossal fine and The Tower of London???

All too soon, time was running out and, just our luck, Brian and I met up with two lovely American women from Scarsdale, New York who were on a Euro-Tour. We dashed off to the Olympic Pool with them for all day and, as we departed, promised to meet them in London later (we did do so). I said a sad goodbye to Santino and he almost wept at our departure, aided by 32 Cognacs he had taken during the day! Soon, Rome was fading into the haze as we headed for the dreaded Autostrada again. Approaching The Alps, we stopped for our last cheap petrol, gazing far ahead to ominous thunderclouds curling above the mountains. John slammed his door and the glass shattered into fragments! We found a plastic binliner and tried to hold back the deluge but, it was useless as the right-side passengers and driver got soaked to the skin and we climbed higher and higher towards the thunder. Without warning, lightning flashed just in front of the car, almost blinding us all! The noise was horrendous and created real fear inside us. Small wonder that the man at the toll booth had shook his head: Crazy English again! We pressed onwards and almost ran into a large boulder (bigger than a car!) which had recently hurtled down and had pounded the roadway, denting it by at least a few inches. We halted and discussed the merits of going ahead as an avalanche of thunder and lightning struck out across the mountain and the car trembled with the incredible noise. In the vain hope that things always get better, we went forward, saturated to the skin, the car coughing itself onward up the slippery road, thousands of feet in the air. Finally, we made it over the top: no-one else was on the road either way and we had crossed the Alps alone that day. Obviously, the majority of travellers had a great deal more sense than we had and we drifted down into a valley, streams gushing torrents on each side, the trees and fields sparkling in the summer rain. Looking back, the view did not seem so dramatic at all and we lit a fire and put on the last of 'The Beans" and they all sizzled away as we attempted to dry out a little. A tyre hissed and the car sank to the ground: continental roads ate up tyres in those days and general moans and groans accompanied the unloading of the boot to reach the tyre-jack. We set off towards Belgium and France and were hungry again as we approached the coast....a farm beckoned in the sunset's rays. Our broken French seemed to tell the lady that we needed bread and eggs; she pointed across the yard to an amazing sight. A rusting, wrecked Sherman tank with American markings clearly visible which served as a chicken-hut! Hens sprang out from inside this metal-monster and straw flew about the yard as the lady groped around for eggs inside the hulk. Battle-damage showed clearly on one side and I couldn't help but think of the brave soldiers who had fought in this machine....what an inglorious end to it all.

Once more in England, I felt distinctly miserable as the M1 Motorway came into view. Summer rain lashed the repaired window and the road to the North looked incredibly bleak and endless. The chill of a 'British Summer' hit me and we all talked of our idea to return next year: I wanted to go back immediately! Those crazy times occupied my thoughts....would I _ever_ have times like that again in my life or was this THE time of my life? My first adventure with the guitar was completed, I could only wonder what the future had in store for me. Little did I know that it was going to be more amazing and adventurous than I could ever imagine.

DARK, SATANIC MILLS....

Although music had been part of my life since the age of six, I never felt that it could or would become my sole source of income until well into my teens. Even then, it took months of prodding and persuasion to modify my attitude. Living near those Dark, Satanic Mills leaves a mark, an invisible mark and the thought of it all evokes memories of those old black-and-white epics like Sons & Lovers, Billy Liar and Saturday Night & Sunday Morning. Born to work, born to lose some may say. Certainly in some regions, you have to study and work extremely hard to cut some ground and often, the only way to progress is to move on to new pastures.

At work, I met Sam. He had a Stay-At-Home existence. At the age of 68, he had been allowed back into work due to depression (on half-pay). He sat all day, cutting rough edges off electronic components for the firm, bored to death, little to look forward to. I sat near him one day and asked him about his life: he lived alone, no woman, no relatives. In the First World War, he had been just too young to fight and had gone into munitions making shells. Between the wars he had gone into the weaving trade working at the looms. Then came World War Two and, due to his training he went directly into munitions again and did not fight, did not travel. He had heard of my planned trip to Germany with a band and he cautioned me on this....

"Why, Neil, do you want to go there?"

was his frequent question. I asked him what was wrong with Germany and he told me that he did not like German food and the language was difficult. At this point I asked him if he had ever been to Germany....

"No....I've never been out of England!"

I sat looking at him for a while, this elderly, bright-eyed gent who then told me that he had never married because women were too expensive! I finally asked about his own travels; he thought and looked skywards....

"I went to Leeds once."

From that moment, I resolved not to be like Sam, not to let the grass grow under my feet but instead, to go with the flow....whatever the consequences. I didn't want to become a Billy Liar; not me. By the way, why did Billy not dash off with the beautiful Julie Christie? He would have had a much better time, a wilder life by far.

After leaving school, I went straight into industry, light and heavy work combined and, although the experience did have some value, it has left me with many regrets, not least of which is the feeling that I should never even have seen the inside of a factory. Our firm made military and civilian aircraft and later, rockets, and so, this aspect cannot obviously be discussed in detail here. A number of apprentices stood lazing around on that first day including a good mate, Terry and also Norman who was busily showing off a motorbike that had been owned by the famous rider, Geoff

Duke. Our bright, unsullied overalls looked faintly ridiculous: I need not have worried too much about that because soon they would be wrecked and ripped apart in the heavy work to come. On occasion, we made our way up to the noisy workshop above and met many characters there including Jack, whose sole life-purpose seemed to be the seeking out of rats (vermin) and electrocuting them with a 1,000 volt supply. As apprentices, we were expected to learn how things were made and the firm often sent us out to local firms to observe parts being made 'on site' rather than simply accept the end product. So it was that we all climbed into a coach and went off on a 'jolly' to Manchester to see how springs and washers were made. As we approached the factory, a door opened and flames could be seen shooting into the air: Hell's kitchen, I thought. Inside, the stench of burning oil was sickly and I wanted to leave at once. The old floor was stained with oil and so battered that one could see through slits into the room below! People bustled here and there and every now and again, the entire building shuddered, as some far-off monster-machine, crunched and twisted metal. At one point, a pretty, middle-aged lady was feeding steel bars into a roller which viciously snatched the bar and twisted the screeching, squealing metal into the familiar spring shape. She sprayed oil onto the steel and the thrashing bar groaned as it tried to avoid being bent on the roller. As she turned towards me, I noticed that her left arm was chopped off at the elbow and, somehow she managed to hold the tongs with her right arm, feeding the bar in. I shouted to her, asking how long she had been on the work....

"Fourteen years, love....I lost my arm here when one of those bars fill back at me. It could have cut me in half, you know? I'm lucky to be here!"

She was LUCKY to be HERE???? I found her charming and actually quite took a fancy to her but surely, surely she did not like this awful job? The machinery screamed out as we shouted over it and I asked if she was happy doing this work....*"Yes, yes love. I wouldn't do anything else!"* As we walked off, some heavy presses began to thump and grind far away down the line and the whole building shuddered with every blow. Once outside, I glanced back into the almost-Dickensian atmosphere as the flames once more belched out from a huge machine. Is this Life (I pondered) Is this Work....for five days of every stinking week until you retire or maybe get both arms chopped off? I sat on the coach with grave misgivings about the future; not only for that charming lady but also for myself!

Back at the Apprentice Training School, I surveyed the lathes and vices and oil-stained benches and began to reconsider my decision to go into engineering. Soon, my music would offer a chance of a lifetime but, by then, I would be signed as an apprentice for the next five years and, as I stared through the grim security-frosted windows and the bars, a terrible feeling of claustrophobia came over me. I was in a kind of prison....some people did not seem to mind being here, working in the oil and filth; I objected to it all! Each day dragged on, broken only by the chats with Terry, my best mate and John. We had formed a group with Keith and Michael and wanted to make the Big Time. But for now, it was back to work and soon I was sent off to the worst place in the camp: the Filing Section under Jack's supervision. There, a new entrant would be given a dirty, misshapen block of metal and within a few days, this had to become one half of a pair of pliers, made purely by sawing and filing for hours on end, each day. The work was hard, and blisters appeared within hours of starting the filing and both shoulders and back took the strain. By the third day, my blisters had broken open and blood ran down the files; it made no difference. I had to wrap rags around the file-ends to actually hold on through the pain and other guys had similar problems. The gloomy, underground atmosphere, enhanced by poor fluorescent lights brought home a 'Gulag' quality to me and Jack prowled around, checking for cheaters; anyone using emery paper or a stone to brighten the finish on a job.

Eventually, I decided to cheat. On the main workshop up top, I had friends on the grinders and I took my lump of metal up in secret and had the surface reduced. The gleaming metal looked fine, the problem was how to disguise the grinding process. I threw the metal down, stood on it with my boots, scraped it along the floor but the bright surface shone back

MICHAEL & THE HUNTSMEN, November, 1963.
This group made quite a name all over Lancashire then. From the left, John, Michael, Keith, Terry and Neil with Fender guitars, 1962 models. (Photo John Moulton collection, courtesy Bolton Evening News)

even more! Arriving back in Stalag-Luft 100, I clamped the block into my vice and rasped away for ages to no good effect. Harder and harder I pressed into the metal, cursing and muttering under my breath, I failed to notice Jack skulking up behind me....

"Ah Ahhhhh! What's all this then?"

he cried out as he unfastened the vice. Taking out an eyepiece, he minutely studied the surface of my work and turning to me with a twisted smile, he clamped the block in my vice and went for a big hammer. He battered my work over and over, bending the almost-finished job totally out of shape and threw it into the Scrap Bin and brought me a new block of unfinished steel. I was ordered to start again, from scratch; no mercy.

At sixteen-plus, I began to really learn about life and hard work. The days were long and, even on machines, the work took all of our energy. Sometimes, there would be accidents, horrific ones too and once, I almost lost my arm as the lathe caught my sleeve and whipped my hand around the metal job. After a year, I moved out into the main works and was immediately transferred to another factory miles away. The start time of 7.30am was hard to make at such distances and the days dragged on and on until the finish time at 5.30pm. More and more I began to feel that I had made a great error in my choice of profession and my music began to interfere with the job too. A spell in the Drawing Office helped me to settle down and there was the compensation of meeting some very attractive girls who generally looked down on us 'lowly' Shop-Floor people. This was short lived because I was transferred again; to Heavy Plant Maintenance. Work with a big W started there!

Battery Duty was first on the menu and young lads would go out to check every battery in the place, an acid-bottle trundled along behind. The following week, my mother shouted upstairs to me....

"Neil: your overalls have fallen into little pieces!"

Sure enough, holes had appeared everywhere and we puzzled it out. Of course....the Battery Acid! I had been wiping my fingers onto the cloth and the acid had eaten my overalls. End of that job for me. Many of the men were ex-RAF fitters and were great at their jobs. Frank was quite literally built like Desperate Dan, an ex-RAF airman from the War, he almost always had huge lads to help him out. His 'Toolbox' was a standing joke in the workshop; only Frank could lift the damn thing! With one hand, he would pick it up like a baby and put it on a trolley. I dreaded the day when I had to carry 'The Box'....the day came. Just after 7.30am, Frank told me to get the box onto a trolley. With both hands, I struggled as everyone stood around, smirking at the comedy of it all. Frank barked out more orders....

"Go and get the Double-Extension Ladder....Now!"

he shouted. I was mortified. These enormous ladders need two persons to carry them safely but Frank expected me to lump the lot! I grappled with the ladder, up on my shoulder as Frank pushed our trolley out into the main workshop and we headed for the main car-park. A lamp had gone in the highest of all of the park lights. Pulling on the ladder, I swung my weight back to take the strain and the ladder went almost upright and then decided to fall down, heading for a row of cars! Frank grabbed the ladder just in time and I put the extension up onto the crossbeam. The tower was incredibly high, the ladder sagged in the middle and, at the top, I noticed only about three inches of wood actually perched over the beam. The wind blew and the ladder shifted leaving about two inches over the bar. The whole event was quite terrifying and I tried to warn Frank but the wind took my words away. I almost ran down the ladder after changing the lamp and told Frank what had happened. He told me that six inches was the minimum overlap needed; I had been extremely lucky to escape!

Our workshop had an oven, a luxury in those days and I decided to bring in my own lunch; Beans. Around 10am, I called back at the oven and put the beans in without opening the tin. Arriving back at 11.50, I heard a bang from the oven but thought little of it. At midday, the oven was opened and my can had exploded; Frank was very pleased, his bacon and scrambled eggs had been enhanced by an extra, free course!

I went on a job with Jack one day, ladders again to fix a fault in a large crane in the Loading Bay; high-level work again. He sent me up the ladder and I had to fumble around in semi-darkness in order to unscrew covers, clamps etc. The noise increased in the Bay as a lorry pulled in and Jack was shouting up to me as I pushed my hand up behind the winder-gear. Jack joined me on the ladder, a most unusual thing to do; he shouted me to stop everything. Handing me his torch, I played the light into the area where I had just been working. To my horror, I saw four thick, bare cables and a skull-and-crossbone sign DANGER 450 VOLTS! This and other signals made me feel that I should have gone into music after all on leaving school. Again, many people were quite happy working with motors bigger than a room or voltages higher than the Electric Chair but I was not so happy and became less so as my 21st birthday approached. I did qualify as an Electrician: Light Current but my heart was not in the job. As I sat one day with Frank, my oil-stained, scarred hands on a sandwich, I ventured to tell him of the near-miss with the overhead crane and the 450 volt supply. He stopped eating for a moment and said....

"Ah lad, you were lucky. One of my mates did that and he had an expanding watch strap on his wrist. Well, it went across the three-phase lines and the bracelet melted into his wrist!"

Frank, a decorated-flyer actually winced as he said this, others sitting eating told him to shut up as he 'expanded' on the expanding-strap tale describing the whole gruesome event.

Listening to stories such as this and sometimes seeing fingers slashed to pieces made me think about my work. I recall too that when a circuit had been wired and finished, the first person to switch on was me (or whoever had done the main work). Sometimes, others would stand away at a 'safe' distance and there was no getting away from it, this could be very dangerous work and a wrong connection, even in a small junction could cause a surge big enough to fry a human being! Even though I later went on to light work, I decided to leave industry forever if possible and, on the final day, I handed in my equipment and went across to see Mr Brown, the Personnel Officer....

"Sit down Mr Smith. I'm sorry to hear that you are leaving us. We did have high hopes for you but, I'm sure that you have made the right choice and are moving on to better things. Which firm will you be going to work for?"

I looked across at him and smiled, telling him about the seedy nightclub where I had been 'moonlighting' for the previous three weeks: he almost fell off his chair!

I'VE GOT RHYTHM,
I'VE GOT MUSIC....

Most people could learn to play a musical instrument if they really had the opportunity to study hard. Playing as an amateur at a basic level is a realistic goal providing the instrument is right for the person involved. Playing at a high level presents numerous problems on all instruments and to achieve national or international standard does require dedication almost on the verge of obsession. Some instruments are inherently more complex simply because they can play more than one note at once and the guitar, with more playable sounds than a grand-piano, falls into this category. I decided to grapple with this wonderful and perplexing piece of wood and if possible, to use it to finance my future. However, for a moment here I must turn back time....way back to the point when music kicked into my life....

Lord Street School is much the same today as when I went there in 1950; nowadays, I only live around the corner! Miss Berry was our Head and also our Music Tutor and one day, she rapped the baton on her lectern after our 'choir' of little tots had groaned through All Things Bright and Beautiful. I was looking at one of the new girls and Miss B saw my head turn and hauled me out to sing....alone!

As I began to sing, her face changed to a smile and I saw the accompanist lean around the piano smiling at me. Miss Berry said that I had an excellent voice and that maybe one day, I would be a singer. And so began ten years of singing in choirs, standing out front, often alone until my voice broke. This in some way directed my path in music and vocal studies play a great part in the life of any professional musician; I got my fill early on! A little later, I went to London and we went along to see the new South Bank Complex. Staring at the giant buildings, we heard some music drifting on a summer breeze and wandered over to an open door to listen. There on stage rehearsing was the skiffle-singer Lonnie Donegan and we all watched until a zealous man shooed us away back into the sunlight. Thirty years later, I too played these great halls but for now, it was onward to secondary school.

Mr Wood was the first master I met in music there and he coached our choir for many hours. Schubert seemed to be one of his favourites and his work continuously introduced us to The Classics; very useful for my later work and something to be grateful for. I passed another examination for a Technical College and at thirteen, headed off on what was essentially a training route for engineers, not musicians. On my first day, I had much to regret. At this all-male school, incredible violence and bullying went on during what was termed 'playtime'....arms were twisted in the railings, iron gates were closed onto juniors by large boys (some near 6ft) who crushed the gates onto the crowd, hands and fingers were burned with matches and other ghoulish tortures awaited. Much of this was done in secret and all-hell faced anyone who happened to be caught in the act. For me, only in the Choir and Music Lessons did peace reign as Mr Taylor force-fed us the music of Handel and Vaughan Williams until we actually enjoyed it all; full marks to him for that. I recalled the many hours singing as the chalk-dust floated by in the shafts of sunlight, never really bored and always under the watchful eye of our master. Festivals and other productions filled our diary and I was later joined by Philip Peet, a superb singer who shared duets with me and became one of my greatest friends and went on to play the organ professionally.

Parallel to these classical exploits, the world at large was becoming aware of an American phenomenon called Elvis Presley and anyone who had a remote resemblance to him was a star....Kevin, my best pal at the time, took on this role. He spent hours in front of the mirror, a picture of Presley in one hand, a comb in the other as he asked for comments on the styling. An old Dansette record-player thumped away in the background as we absorbed the _real_ Elvis P: slap-echo tracks like Mystery Train which featured the great guitar work of the legendary Scotty Moore. All of those ballad-style tracks did not suit us and seemed too much like the music of our parents; drooling, sentimental balladry. Since there was a guitar twanging along on all of the major albums, I wanted a guitar too and Trevor had one for sale, a Hofner 222 and I bought it for the princely sum of two pounds! Pretty soon, I had figured out the chord-boxes and I could strum along to Presley and the rest by the time of my final year at school. Since my college was cocontially a technical-grade school, most artistic things were put on hold and sadly, I never was asked to bring the guitar into class and had to bend my mind to coping with lathes, millers, spanners, etc, etc. I should have known that my destiny was not in engineering the day I sheared off the end of my left thumb; lucky for me, a guitarist does not need this finger-tip! And then another sign came when I dropped a red-hot bar of metal onto the workbench; the old, oil-stained bench blazed into life, flames touching the low ceiling and it was only put out by a quick thinking master nearby.

I have the greatest sympathy now with young people leaving school since my own leaving was a most disjointed, frustrating time. Even though I saw an Employment Officer in the final few months, he was of no value and only offered 'ENGINEERING' or 'THE FORCES' as options for someone like me, a lad straight from the desk. Only when I was with my friends or the girls I used to date did I really feel alive; or when I played my guitar. I was in the top year at school but still, bullying took its toll and I could not wait to leave. The last day in our 'Borstal' saw us running out early, kicking our leather satchels across the yard as a master shouted impotently after our gang. We ran to the local railyards, stupidly jumping on wagons and even dodging in between them literally dicing with death: by an awful coincidence, Kevin was killed during his job at British Rail in such an accident. On that far-off and sunny day, work seemed such a long way off in our minds as we vaulted over railings and the railtracks. Our grubby, little hands got dirtier and dirtier as we larked about like the Famous Five and we ran home, much too late for tea.

During that summer, the temperature rose higher and higher as I strolled about town. School had ended for my year and the little cafes and snack-bars were filled to bursting with youngsters listening to the raunchy sound of Eddie Cochran alongside the somewhat dated sounds of Bill Haley and The Comets. One place just out of town became a hang-out for motor bikers....black leather and boots, girls hanging off the back as they roared off into the distance, often heading for the quite beautiful countryside (Rivington, Lancashire) close by my home. As I sipped a Coke with Ice Cream and Raspberry (worth a try if you've never tried it) the afternoon heat beat down on the Rockers outside and I began to ponder exactly what was in store for me. By September, I was due to start a 5-year stint as an apprentice and yet, somehow another world was beckoning me. The juke-box noise was so invasive, so powerful and so up-to-date that it could not be ignored....and another thing struck me too. At the heart of almost every song was a guitar solo; the jingle-jangle instrument so long overlooked which had become the instrument of the age.

One night during a downpour, I passed an old club and heard noises filtering down from the dance hall above. Climbing the stairs, I came to a desk with an old, bored man sitting on guard and he asked me for a shilling (5p in our money) to enter this 'Rock & Roll Dance' ..to be honest, the whole event seemed beyond his comprehension. The bright lights, the thunder of the drums as Hank Marvin broke into that mega-hit *Apache* and the girls dancing away across the floor in bright dresses, twirling and jiving around their handbags. Very few guys went up to dance but still, the whole event seemed like another world; a world that I wanted to escape into. Other people thought (and still do so) that music was not a 'proper job' but to me, it all gelled and I had to have music in my life. As the guitars echoed across the pounding drums and the girls flashed by, I knew deep inside that Music would get me one day....exactly how it would happen seemed beyond me and remote. I only recall the sadness as the Bop ended and we all shuffled out into the miserable Lancashire night.

Bill and Tom ran a band, an ad-hoc ensemble downtown and eventually they invited me to join them for a rehearsal as they thrashed away in a fog-bound classroom borrowed from the local school. I had to walk almost a mile with my guitar and a little Watkins amplifier and arrived soaked to the skin but happy; this was where it all happened, this was IT. Tom enjoyed having an audience present and would often scour the streets outside for 'listeners'....men, women (especially young women) and even

DOGS came in at times. One evening, he brought in a tramp. The tramp sat there and seemed quite impressed with our show and was even keener when a cup of coffee was forced into his hands. Soon, he drifted off to our ballads only to be rudely awakened by Tom who was expecting a routine critique. The embarrassed look upon his face remains with me as Tom tore into him, grilling him ruthlessly until he could offer no more information having obviously and criminally been asleep, drunk or otherwise rendered incapable during our staggeringly-stupendous Royal Variety warm-up....and the tramp was mercilessly turfed out into the cold and damp. Exitus Musicus Criticus.

This band later drifted apart and I met Keith who already had a guitar and John a good drummer and, along with Terry on bass we formed a group: Lancashire's answer to The Shadows indeed. Local clubs took us on right away and then a superb singer called Michael joined in who, with his cherub-faced looks, completed our line-up by adding Cliff Richard to our outfit. One day, our local council wrote to ask us to front a talent show at our main festival and wanted me to back a couple of local singers. At rehearsals, we all milled about for a while until a local gent called Charles summoned attention and got the show on the road. As we tuned up, the room fell silent as an absolutely gorgeous young woman stepped up on stage. She sang quite well but above all that, her quite stunning good-looks seemed to floor the lads in the audience. Ten years later I met Carol again and we eventually married and had three children.

One day, John the drummer came in with good-bad news: he had been approached by The Falcons, a group with a big name in the North at the time and so, we went into town to 'Have a Jam' as the saying goes. We both got accepted and had to tell the other guys the bad news. Arguments followed but we all remained in touch as The Falcons went on to greater heights.

Although I never felt tired, I was actually running three 'lives' then: work, the electric guitar and the Spanish guitar. My father bought me a disc of Andres Segovia and I was hooked: I little realized that I would meet Segovia many times and would play on the same stages within hours of his own show! I had to find local lessons and also Theory Lessons to learn about Music. Robert Marsh coached me in Theory, a fantastic pianist who at one point played duets with the great Tchaikovsky Prize-Winner, John Ogdon....I needn't say any more. Luckily, in my area I found a pupil of Julian Bream and began serious work on spanish guitar with Michael Strutt. Suddenly, he was offered a job in the musical show Man of La Mancha in London....and then he emigrated to Canada. We met for a final drink at a local pub before he went west....and he took me to task,

"Of course, you do realize that this 'engineering thing' is not for you, don't you? Really Neil, you must STOP IT ALL NOW!"

He was of course correct; I knew this but it had never been pointed out so directly before. Here was a professional telling me to forget work and do my own thing. This may sound easy but when one has been brought up in a general workaday atmosphere, it takes an earthquake to make you move onward and I know that many people grow older in a good 'safe' job and then look back, thinking what might have been. A life in Music was out there and my time had come to decide my future. I took over Michael's pupils and also one concert date he had in Manchester: playing after a Masonic dinner. On the appointed night, I arrived in tuxedo and scanned the hall. The wood-panels looked great for sound and I did not need a microphone. As I made my entrance, a colonel-type blocked me....

"Playing guitar tonight? I hope that you won't be too loud dear chap!"

Looking directly into his eyes, I replied....

"I'm trying to be as loud as I possibly can!"

He looked horrified and exclaimed....

"Good heavens....I say: you must be raving mad!"

Michael was gone and I looked for tuition elsewhere in the UK, frequently going to London to see John Duarte at his home or Julian Byzantine (of the Royal College) and also Adele Kramer (of the Guildhall). Each one of these noted tutors had contact with the greatest players and they all helped me in a variety of ways. Adele was quite severe and strict: she would often tap time with her ruler and would sometimes tap my fingers if a fault occurred. Her strong pre-War Austrian accent had not vanished and one day, I spoke to her about her work with the great Miguel Llobet, a virtuoso from the old school of guitar. Around her room, the faded prints told her story and she drew my attention to an ancient classroom scene....

"Here I am also and here....the boy stood beside me, do you know who that is ? It is Adolf Hitler!"

Taken aback, I studied the print closely, Adele with her ringlets and a boy with sloping hair to one side, a rather menacing stare already showing on his young face. Adele had been his friend at school and then they lost touch. When he became Chancellor of Germany, she heard many reports of terrible events and decided to move away forever, eventually settling in London. I asked her about him....

"He was quite an ordinary boy, nothing special but I do recall that he was a very good artist, his pictures were quite nice. Yes, an ordinary boy of the kind who would keep frogs in his pocket."

So much for Adolf Hitler and his connection with the guitar....and frogs!

Due to my obvious connections with the electric guitar, I was perhaps a natural choice for the job of demonstrating the first commercial plug-in-electric Classical Guitar by Takamine. Since this had all of the links with the 'electric' guitar, few orchestras would take me on at first and so it fell to the Blackpool Symphony Orchestra and their conductor, Robert

Atherton (father of David Atherton). On a bitter winter's night at Norbreck Castle, I set up the amplifier within the orchestra to play the great Rodrigo Concerto....puzzled expressions and frowns all around. My old pal Hugh de Camillis came along and he sat in the audience; we had worked out a set of signals to tell me if the guitar was too loud or too soft and the idea worked well,...so well in fact that I asked Hugh to go to the Royal Festival Hall in London a few years later and to use the same signal-code; point up for more volume, down for less, keep still if all was fine. At this enormous venue, I failed to take into account the 3,000 plus persons sitting around Hugh and the glaring spotlights too! For the first few minutes, I stared long and hard out at the crowd, blinking my eyes then playing and looking out again. I did eventually catch sight of Hugh, sat there totally immobile, frozen in his seat in case he made a wrong move! The things we have to do to make money!

The real day-to-day struggles of an artist's life need not be recalled here except to say that to try to make a living via music can be so very, very arduous and even ruinous. For years and years, I practised day and night. Bookings were few and my electric guitar came to my aid making money. My wife Carol was very helpful and she wrote by hand hundreds of letters to clubs, halls, etc, etc. We got FOUR replies and only two concerts! Small wonder then that people despair and lose hope and, having given the best years to study, find a way out by suicide. Even today some artists take this option or sink into the abyss of drink or drugs. Maybe I have not been over-successful but then, few people are. I have lived a full and rewarding life as these pages bear witness, living at the sharp end, pulling few punches.

At long last, in the 70's serious concerts came my way and this lifted me beyond the dreaded time-zone where I had considered giving it all up. Jointly with Manchester Guitar Circle, I promoted a few concerts in the Free Trade Hall....to be more precise, the Upper Hall which has a few hundred seats. I booked a date but also cautioned the Manager that if a rock-band or a brass-band booked the main hall, then I would cancel due to the sound transfer. I sat in the Green Room on that night and noises outside became so annoying that I had to go out. A big, jolly-faced man in a Guards uniform walked by lugging a massive drum: I grabbed his arm to ask his purpose....

"Coldstream Guards mate: a massed bands gig. We're doing the 1812....with cannons."

The Coldstream, The Irish and The Welsh Guards <u>and</u> Cannons, all underneath my hall!!!! I found the Manager; a new man who knew nothing of my plight. On stage, very little came through until I heard the Imperial Anthem striding out below and the boom of a cannon shook the whole building. People in the front row covered their smiles and again, the guns boomed out, the bells and chimes clanged....all through my quietest piece!

Almost everyone in my audience was smiling and, naturally, I could not keep my face straight.

About the same time as this ridiculous episode, another crazy event loomed up in my life. I was asked to take part in a national promotion campaign for a new sherry from Spain; Don Cortez by name and many readers may recall the TV/radio/press buildup for this brand. I was booked to play at almost thirty big hotels across England where I played guitar as two very attractive Spanish waitresses served FREE sherry and then FREE food and then danced for a few minutes at the close. On the first night, all went brilliantly and the tour-manager handed me a full list of the venues which made up our tour. As I scanned the list, one name stood out from the rest; a large, violent, scruffy hotel in Manchester where I had seen bottles and glasses thrown through mirrors. Quickly, I told the manager about this unsuitable venue and he agreed to contact HQ to deflect this possible nightmare. He did contact the company and the message came back; no dice, we had to play ALL dates as listed. The date loomed up ahead….a Friday night of all nights to make matters worse.

I arrived early along with the dancers and began to set the room area as the food arrived and cases of sherry. By 7.40pm, we had set up and I strummed a few chords on my guitar as the girls listened, waiting for the manager to arrive. When we had entered the building, two or three tramp-like men had leered at the girls and I warned the women to watch out this night, like no other. As we waited upstairs, one of these unshaven, unkempt people crept up the steps and observed me playing; he asked what was going on and the girls told him! His eyes lit up like diamonds and a big smile came across his grubby face and without invitation, he walked up to the counter and picked up a schooner of sherry and guzzled it down….licking his lips, he shot off downstairs. Shortly afterwards, a group of his friends came up and went directly to the bar, tippling drinks down at full speed. The manager suddenly arrived and watched with horror as these 'guests' plundered the food with their dirty fingers and, at the top of th stairs three women appeared who would all have made a sleazy-woma look distinctly posh. They too joined in and the manager called a halt but was all too late; more people came upstairs and crammed the bar, or man stepped past me and went around the bar, stealing a bottle and shovi it inside his coat, another man threatened the manager with a fist to his face and then another man took a whole case of the sherry away as his friend grabbed a whole chicken! The place was in uproar, no one wanted to assist the poor manager as he risked life and limb to deal with these wild-men and he ran downstairs looking for the bouncers. So many people filled the room that it was hard for these heavies to push everyone out but, by around 8.15, the place was empty and it looked as if a tornado had gone through. Bottles lay on their side, glugging sherry out onto the tables, glasses were smashed all round, decorations pulled down and the manager sat with his head in his hands. Yes, I did say it to him…."I told you so!"

Beyond this mayhem, more serious tours and trips came in and I did quite a lot of TV and radio, records too and a chart-entry with Lisa Stansfield called 'Your Alibis' and I at last got a booking with a big outfit; The City Birmingham Symphony Orchestra directed by the great Marcus Dods. Marcus was a wonderful character, he was an ex-Battle of Britain pilot who often flew himself to bookings by private plane. After the concert, he asked me to play the Rodrigo at the Queen Elizabeth Hall in London! I practised like a crazy man and it was worth it because Dods booked me yet again and then at the Royal Festival Hall and, finally, at the Barbican Hall shortly after the opening in 1982. My event was part of a Gala Weekend which included two of the greats: Segovia and Rostropovich, two of my idols! To make the gala more special, His Excellency The Spanish Ambassador came to my concert and HRH Prince Charles and Princess Diana attended the Rostropovich evening. The whole area buzzed with security as we all opened and closed our instrument cases many times for checking. My wife and both children travelled down by rail just in time to see a very successful event. Backstage, I stood with Marcus and he warmly shook my hand: I felt elated. Maybe, just maybe this was the pinnacle of my work here in the UK. I had played on Radio 1,2,3 and 4 and many local channels, on BBC and ITV many times, had made records and had played at almost all of the big festivals and now the big London halls too. Caroline and Katy, my children ran along the vibrant corridors towards me and held my hands as I savoured this moment. Here in such a hallowed place, royalty en-route, distinguished musicians and colleagues milling around, my youngest daughter suddenly looked up at me and said….

"Dad: I've got a hole in my knickers!"

MEETING A STAR
A special show for a cancer fund with Julie Goodyear (Bet Lynch from Coronation Street) and John Turner, Recorder player.
courtesy, Sunday Mirror

SWINGING SIXTIES

The 60's have become something of a cult-time these days. Many celebs talk about it with passion, many youngsters take on the image or even the dress of that time, the music, the style; everything seems at this late date to have become larger than life, more fashionable even than it was then. So many things happened to me during that formative time and they need complete description now and so, I will return for a moment to the 60's and replay those scenes for all to see.

Being fifteen in 1960 certainly put me right on the line of demarcation; older people wore 'Flappers' (wide trousers) and had short hair, tweed suits, etc, etc. Perhaps the only thing I had in common with such people was an interest in Classical music alongside Pop. Everything seemed to be changing, revolving....in the right direction: whatever that was. And for me, life would bring romance, music, drink, good food, travel, and work to the fore. Sometimes, all of these would happen almost at once, the same time-space, the same evening even. This world-rebellion against the Old Order seemed self-managed, self-orientating, self-motivated as people became more and more affluent and less and less concerned with past rules and regulations and style. But sometimes The Line was crossed....

Tom worked in our local cinema as Projectionist and, during the intermission, his job was to play records as the advertisements drolled on and on about nothing new. Suddenly one night, the record stopped dead: Victor Sylvester's Dance Orchestra playing a Tango. There was silence for a few seconds and then came the raunchy sounds of the guitars of the Everly Brothers....the whole place buzzed, feet tapped as the music belted out the message. Mr Rimmer owned the cinema and I saw him at the front of the stalls: he was not amused and virtually ran his way to the Projection Box! Suddenly, the record scratched its way off the turntable and silence descended once more. Then out came the smooth, Bryllantine sound of the Sylvester Orchestra once again as some of the audience booed. I looked back up from the stalls and saw Tom making his way out of the Projection Room: he had crossed The Line....the Old Order did not want our noisy, guitar-driven music....ever.

Transport is the eternal problem of the musician, even for the rich and famous. In the 60's the undisputed King of Transport was a Bedford Dormobile van, complete with sliding doors, VERY small heater and, if the band did not have the cash, a view of the road THRU the floor! Sometimes on old vans, the doors would actually slide off into the road or the back doors refused to close or open at critical times. So it was that I went with John and the others to play in Salford and the van gave up en route. Stopped on a corner illegally it was not long before a constable appeared and he began asking questions about the van. This event delayed us considerably and, as we drove off, I heard Graham (the driver) mutter a famous Salford saying...."Bloody Ecilops!" I pondered on this all night as we played on and on and then ventured to ask Graham what he had actually meant. ECILOP is actually Police said backwards and is a slang word used around that area.

Graham was not just our driver and pal; he enjoyed being a 'minder' for the band. On one night, I was glad that he travelled with me to my home. The van had, as usual, let us down and all members had to go home by any route/means. We both decided to catch the train (they ran all night then, believe it or not) and we boarded a grim, suburban non-corridor train at about midnight. As the train rumbled into a grime-covered platform, a huge man stepped into our carriage, almost fell down onto me and then collapsed in a corner. Graham had been a commando and could make short work of anyone; tonight was his moment. The newcomer looked around and, seeing Graham's menacing expression, turned to me and asked....

"Got a cigarette man?"

I said that I did not smoke....this seemed to annoy him and he stood up, well over six-foot in height, came over to me and grabbed my lapels! He repeated his question as he shook me: I raised my arms. Suddenly, there was a scuffle and the man was on his back, on the floor with Graham's foot on his neck! The man, almost choking gurgled out the word "Sorry!" as he lay there, helpless. Graham told him that he had to get off at the next stop; the man protested. Graham pulled down the window and said....

"All right: you can go out NOW!"

The man screamed at this as the train thundered on into the blackness and, for a moment, I could see that Graham meant what he had said. Relenting, Graham pinned him down until the station, hauled him up, opened the door and threw him onto the platform. Shouting abuse, the guy skulked off into the shadows as Graham watched to make sure that he failed to get the train. The whole situation seems, even today, not very pleasant, not legally-nice but, in such circumstances, what is the alternative?

I began to move into the nightlife of Manchester and, in particular the clubs of Moss Side, often associated these days with a variety of problems, not least drugs. There was something exciting, magical and daring even about a night out in the city then. Bright lights twinkled in the pubs as the piano jangled out a tune, in other bars, the juke-box roared away with the latest American hit and over in Liverpool, a few bands began to make a name nationally. Into this world I came as an innocent and fortunately, I missed out on some of the most bizarre features of such a lifestyle. Of that particular period, some nights stand out in my mind these days. Once, I arrived at the club very early: the smoke still hung in the air from the previous night, cleaners shuffled around with brooms and the smell of stale liquor was quite overpowering. I walked on into our usual 'Dressing-Room'....a kind of office, walls filled with addresses, business cards, photos and the odd abusive word. As I threw the door open, I stopped dead: there stood in front of me was a naked woman, her back turned towards me. Without any embarrassment at all she swivelled round to face me saying....

"Well, what the hell are you staring at you......................!"

I was sixteen and to be honest, very naive, and not only her appearance startled me....she actually swore like a trooper. I closed the door and the organist told me (belatedly) to use another room and as we pottered along the corridor, I told him of my experience; he said "Ee lad, thee has got a lot to learn for sure!" He was right of course and the Music Business was going to teach me. At that same club one night, a man with a strong Liverpudlian accent approached me and gave me a business card, asking at the same time if I was with the band permanently. When I confirmed this, he proceeded to outline the most amazing offer musically-speaking. He was linked with various bands from Merseyside who were about to go to Germany on tour and they needed a guitarist. He was much impressed by my playing and he needed a Dep-guitarist....in layman's terms, a stand-in player for all and any sick band member. Recall that in those days, groups did not mime like so many trashy bands of today and so a full compliment of players was essential all of the time. He talked quietly and furtively: groups do not like members being 'poached' and it can lead to animosity and violence. He mentioned a few names....The Dakotas, The Merseybeats and others including The Beatles. My job involved mastering every intro and solo for each group and then, if necessary, I had to jump on stage as a deputy. Incredible as it may seem, special matching clothes would be made for me for each band and with some groups I would have to wear a wig for effect.

I went off with his card with two weeks to consider the idea. At home, my father could not believe his ears; I had just signed a 5-year contract as an apprentice. This clash of events was unfortunate since it involved a buying-out fee of £1,000 (a terraced-house cost around £1,000 then) and so, time went by and the deadline expired. Easy to be wise after the event but, in those days, few people around guessed accurately what was about to happen. Should I have gone? I guess maybe so in view of my later career in Music but, we all make mistakes: BIG ones sometimes!

Later I deputized with many trios and small outfits during that Manchester period and some famous stars of the day were on stage; The Kaye Sisters, Matt Munro, etc, etc. We had to read 'The Dots' (music) which varied from well-scored items to scruffy, hand-scribbled scores in which half of the accompaniments had to be virtually improvised due to lack of clarity. Often, complete tunes were done off-the-cuff, especially if someone was running out of numbers, 'live' on-stage. Sometimes however, an act would bring along precise notation, fully-timed with stops and starts of the most complex kind and these had to be fully rehearsed to go exactly with the action occurring on-stage. One such act went by the name of Stromboli, a professional fire-eater/strong man. He came to the club in the late afternoon and it emerged that at one point in his show, a huge rope would be tied around his neck and several men would pull on each side as he resisted the pressure choking him! It went well all week until Friday night when the club was full of serial-drinkers. As usual, I stood behind Stromboli as he flexed his muscles, ate fire, bent iron bars and did the routine very competently. Soon, drinkers crawled out of the crowd to take part in the great 'strangling' event. At each side they stood (or rather, swayed) Stromboli looked left at the drummer and the roll began. Under strict orders, the drums went loud as the rope tightened and then, as the trick ended, Stromboli clapped his hands for the 'pullers' to stop. This night, they did not stop and a real strangling was in the offing. I saw his neck sag inwards and he fell sideways as the drunks dragged him around the stage! Pandemonium broke out as various rescuers ran on stage and, for the first time ever I heard....

"*Is there a doctor in the house?*"

Fortunately, there was and many nurses too since this club was close by the residences.

One particular club had a great variety of clientele: wrestlers, dealers in this or that, ladies to suit all tastes and....something else. Graham sat chatting to some women as I played on stage one night and one woman was particularly keen to meet me. They were easily the best lookers in the entire room and Graham called me over as I left the stage door. My 'lady' was certainly beautiful, blonde, long, shapely legs very attractive by any standard. We all chatted away, looking longingly into each others' eyes and Graham went off to the bar for a round of drinks. He never returned! I waited and waited, dumb with embarrassment but he simply stood at the bar and occasionally signalled for me to go over to him. After what seemed like eternity, I plucked up enough courage to walk off and over to the bar. Graham looked shifty and glanced around him and said....

"*Those women we are with are NOT women....they are men!*"

Today, this may seem common or quaint; in 1962, it was an eye-opener.

As the Sixties went on, I progressed onto other forms of music; cabaret, dance-band, jazz and country & western. This field has some of the finest guitar-players in the world and modern 'Country Guitar' is in no way easy or low level. I joined a band run by Billy, a good outfit with great characters. On our first gig, I stood behind stage waiting and saw the bass-player put on dark glasses. This can be normal due to the blinding effect of spotlights on stage. Once on stage, the guitarist was 'led' over to the microphone and the band kicked off. At the first opportunity, we were all introduced and my new companion turned out to be Blind Jimmy....a huge cheer rose from the audience. Later backstage, he took off his glasses and went outside to play Bingo! And he dutifully returned later and donned the glasses; there is no business like show business!

Once with this same outfit, we played a job in town and, halfway into our first number, a man walked on stage and simply grabbed the microphone from Billy! He announced....

"Ladies and Gentlemen....the pies have come. Potato on the left and steak on the right. Onions and condiments are on the bar. Thank you."
Our new bassman was Alan; tall and unfriendly and he stopped playing and went off-stage and grabbed this man, shaking him by the lapels! He was a Committee Man and this ended our booking and the prospect of any more work at that club....unless we sacked Alan!

The late nights began to play havoc with my day work and although I yearned for a pro-music opportunity, there were certain worrying features of this lifestyle apparent to me. One night, I sat with others at a table and a large fight erupted next to our party. As I stood up to move away, a member on our table grabbed my arm and told me to sit down. Without batting an eye, he stood up and pulled out a gun! Picking up a chair, he banged it loudly on the floor until the fighting halted....the battlers shuffled outside, humbled by such grand fire-power. On another occasion, some foolish, bragging men started a fight in the club <u>after</u> a Pro-Wrestling match!!!! They were demolished by a gang of gigantic wrestlers in full-flight, an awesome spectacle. At another club, two bus conductors in uniform (male and female) entered very late in the evening and they drank and smooched around, eventually spilling their change all over the floor. A riot broke out as members swarmed onto the floor grabbing money as the conductors tried in vain to halt this highway-robbery! Eventually, the opportunity came for me to leave my day-job and I started working at a club with Terry, Keith and Eddie until 2am, six nights a week. Many future TV stars came and drifted through there and it seemed quite permanent to me: one night changed all that.

On stage one evening, a man stepped from the audience and pushed a business card into my hand with the words....

"Give me a ring....I need a good player like you, ok?"
He vanished smartly and I wandered into our dressing room in the break....there waiting for me was the club owner and his biggest 'bouncer' glaring at me! They closed the door for a 'private' chat and I sat down as the bouncer glowered, flexing his arms as he did so. The owner broke the terrible silence....

"So Neil, I have heard that you may be thinking of leaving here?"
I denied this, shaking my head as I did so and watching the bouncer more and more. The boss-man went on in a sardonic tone....

"We have been good to you Neil (I nodded) and we don't want things to become a problem....you understand me?"

In saying this, he looked over his shoulder at the bruiser behind him. I repeated my rather pathetic excuses and he seemed convinced; as he left the room, he turned back towards me saying....

"I'm giving you more money, from tonight OK? This is to help you make up your mind....understand?"

I nodded and felt enormous relief that no blows had been aimed my way: for the moment! Weeks went by and I knew that I had to move on eventually and so, hesitantly, I made the call to the number on the card, called in to see about the other job and then went home to consider it all. Later that night, I arrived to play at the club; and also to hand in my notice! Again, I met the owner in the dressing room and I told him my news. To my surprise, he quickly thought about it and told me....

"Find me another player like yourself soon....then GO!"

Two weeks later, I found someone else and they took over....thankfully.

The 60's careered onwards and so did I. I married for the first time, we both saw it as a big mistake and were divorced under the new 'Quickie-Style' decrees in 1969. Once more, I was single, free and without any real responsibilities. Soon, I was working on stage for big organizations like Top Rank and Mecca. Eventually I joined the Mecca Dance Band in town, met up with Maurice and Barry the other guitar players on stage, and thus began a series of incidents of which I can mention but a few.

The stage at Bolton Palais revolved: a bouncer used to hand-turn a wheel and this would move the mechanism under the platform. As he turned and turned, the band started to play and revolve but, the brake had to be applied gently. Often, the guy turning would be in a foul mood and would turn us rapidly and throw on the brake sending us spinning across the stage, music stands collapsing everywhere as chaos erupted. The quartet on the reverse side-of-stage had simmering disputes with our band and insults, cat-calls and offensive words flew back and forth across the blaring music....the dancers were in the main oblivious to this. One night, I saw a lovely woman in the crowd; she smiled and I waved and so she kept watching me from afar. I said nothing to the band but, in the interval, I threw down my jacket and dashed out into the ballroom; she was there waiting! We danced and she gave me her phone number. All too soon, the magic break ended and I went backstage to get ready. As we waited, the door burst open and the Manager strode in....

"Who has been dancing outside? I want to know now! This is instant dismissal!"

I did not know but Mecca had a very strict rule; I had broken it. The entire band stood in silence waiting for me to own up and just in time, a bouncer ran in; a big fight had broken out in the hall and the Manager left us. The fight saved my job!

The work took up six nights a week and went on late. Such activities tend to draw a band together socially and we often stayed back or went on to a club into the early hours or even sat with the cleaners who searched the floor for coins; 4,000 people on a Saturday night can drop a lot of money. Just like any 'normal' job, we had outings and soon the Easter Trip came along and we all decided to go to the Isle of Man for a day out. Leaving from Liverpool, we drank like crazy on the cheap liquor but, as the boat began to rock, we were all ill. Arriving at Douglas drunk in the afternoon, our rowdy crowd made for Yates Wine Lodge and there began to drink champagne on draught.

After a while, we went outside and sat down. Eventually, I looked at my watch and it was ten minutes BEYOND the leaving time for the boat! We ran and ran down the street and, as expected, the boat was away from dock, our pals waving goodbye and roaring with laughter. Neil, Barry and Maurice marooned for at least 24 hours! We scraped together cash from our pockets to buy some chips in newspaper and headed for the beach. As darkness fell, we noticed a fire to our left and, as we approached could hear some real hippies chanting out music to the guitar. We joined in and of course, when they found out our 'trade' the guitars were handed over and a few hours went by eating, drinking, playing and laughing about our plight. Cider was brought out and whisky too and soon, my head was spinning; I wandered off, away, off into the distance and then….BLANK.

A telephone rang, terribly bold and brash, almost against my ear! I picked up the handset very gently….

THE YEAR OF 1969.
With my Gibson Stereo Guitar, pointed shoes and my green van. People used to say I had long hair then....really?
Courtesy, Jeff Wilkinson

"Your alarm call sir! You should just have enough time to get the 9 o'clock boat."

I peered around the palatial room. Fully clothed, I fell out of bed and opened the curtains to see the blinding sunlight. Dishevelled, I almost tottered downstairs to the foyer and spoke to a man at the desk. Yes, he recalled my arrival at around 3.30am, I had seemed fine and had turned out my coat-lining in front of him to reveal some money; enough to pay for the best room at the Casino! I half-ran and half-staggered back to the boat departure; Barry and Maurice were quite worried following my sudden trip off to nowhere and we all boozed away as the boat chugged home. On arrival, Barry had to explain his absence to his irate wife: she appeared as a vision behind the glass of the front door, frying pan in hand! Barry came back to my place for a while.

About that time, I sported a rather worn-out Ford van which carried my gear around the place from town to town. I finished very late one night at the dance hall (due to trying to date a cleaning lady) as the rest of the band made their way across town to a new late-night venue. I got into my van and set off on the normal route. Unknown to me, the intended route had been pedestrianised THAT DAY! Onwards I went, bumping over some huge ramps, just avoiding some badly placed signs and some very large plant pots blocking the way. The Town Hall clock glared down at me from the right but everything else seemed rather strange and out of place. A policeman sauntered across the concrete towards me and he gave a little salute with his baton as I trundled past him! Arriving at the club, I bored everyone with the story until someone clicked on to what had occurred. My van was actually identical in size and colour to the Council vans used for gardening etc. The policeman had obviously taken me for a council worker on business! Had he known my error, he might not have saluted me so politely.

Innumerable social and musical events made up the late 60's for me. Often, I would find myself stuck without the promised transport miles from home, once walking almost a dozen miles in sub-zero conditions at night without a coat! Once, part of the band drove away with the van full of women, leaving me and another member to walk or get a cab. At one particular sailing club, cars and vans parked on the slipway due to the parking overspill. When the dance ended at around 2am, a drunken man emerged and, sensible as it may seem, he handed the car keys to his sober wife. She however, was not used to the gearbox on the car and threw it into reverse! Down the ramp it went, into the black, gurgling water as the exhaust entered first! Panic took hold and she could not stop as the gleaming vehicle sank lower and lower, the woman looking more and more terrified with every passing moment. Eventually, she stopped, men ran into the water to pull open the doors and the car was abandoned until daylight. On another occasion, I played on Christmas Eve with a band on a late gig beyond closing time. As midnight approached, I became aware of a policeman standing in the outer doorway. Almost at once, his sergeant stepped up on stage….

"Are you aware that the Landlord does not have a late licence? Stop playing or you will all be arrested!"

We stopped and the whole event ended in confusion due to some missing paperwork at the Licensing Offices. Fighting broke out which ended up with the pub 'Bouncer' getting nicked! Once, some friends planned a small party; it lasted THREE DAYS & NIGHTS, none-stop! Bizarre, but true.

On occasion, a band could be signed up for a major tour or could just happen to link up with a famous soloist or singer. One such night we were due to appear with the very famous American rock-singer Gene Vincent. Sadly for us (and the fuming audience) Vincent and his band had driven hundreds of miles in the wrong direction to a town with a similar name….several counties away! That particular venue was well known locally for promoting big 'Rock' events and one night they set up a special show with five live bands. Even though we reduced the chaos by only having two drumkits on stage, the whole area looked like something out of the NASA space programme as wires and leads crossed everywhere and none of the guitar players would sacrifice his amplifier and sound by plugging in to another set-up. Eventually, the whole thing got started, we were second band on and as we closed, up to the front came a set of real 'groupies'….people who seemed really high and they swayed and chanted as the next group got started on what seemed to be non-commercial material; in truth, most of the audience found it all puzzling and only the crowd in front were taken by the event, Strange to think of such a reaction to one of the world's most famous bands today….Pink Floyd no less!

Playing the guitar can be an exhilarating experience in public….to quote the late Jimi Hendrix,

"Music is a safe kind-of-high"

and I think that most players could perhaps agree with that. The actual learning process is far-removed from this however as the would-be 'rocker' struggles away with a very complex instrument, almost turning into an anorak-stereotype, alone in a room at home with only discs and photos of the famous and the great players he or she may never equal or meet. To actually see or meet someone who has achieved fame is like finding gold to such prospectors and people can dine out on the story for years. In one of the many bands I worked in, we were fortunate to be offered a residency at a large club in the city. Some well-known acts appeared there (P.J. Proby, Duane Eddy, etc) and one night, I went in early to change my strings. As I entered the dimly lit hall, I heard some superb rock-guitar sounds emerging from the dressing room. As I wandered in, the guy stopped playing and nodded towards me asking about my guitar. We sat chatting as I tied on the strings and I found out that he was a deputy player for the top-of-the-

33

bill that night and had whizzed up from London to help....Jimmy Page was his name, later to find much fame in Zepplin. Strange who you meet in a dilapidated dressing room on a rainy night in the Swinging Sixties. Guitarists tend to either hoard or fall in love with a particular guitar, the obvious instrument in the 60's was a Fender Stratocaster (see photo-group) and like so many other players, I had my share of these superb instruments. Gibson guitars tended to be favoured by 'Jazz-Players' and these gave a clear, and yet resonant tone, not quite as steel-like as the Fender but still, well worth paying a great deal of money for. I eventually bought a Gibson 345 Stereo model from 1962 (shown in this collection) and along with a Marshall amplifier, I felt ready to take on all comers. My main band with this guitar was a Mecca dance-band at Bolton, a great outfit with experienced players from all over the North and also players from the great Atlantic liners who had settled into a life on-shore. The leader was Les Moss, an incredible character whose sarcasm had to be heard to be believed. Saturday night was party-nite there as some 3,000 plus people drank and danced the night away and the actual power needed to cut through the density of the crowd was almost painful for the members of the band. Occasionally, Les would wander across the stage and would bend low shouting to me....

"Is that on full? Is that how loud that thing will go?"

And then without warning, he would turn every control clockwise and smile as the awesome sound burst out of the amp and he would back off, giving an approving nod as he did so.

Before I actually joined the band, I had seen them in action and had noticed a very attractive female-vocalist (as they used to be called) on stage with the band and, from afar, I wanted to meet her and to get to know her. Suddenly, there I was, on stage, right alongside her playing with a top band! Every Sunday was special because our band would deputize for the Phil Moss Band at the Ritz Ballroom, Manchester, probably the premier dance-venue in the North at the time. On arriving at the hall, we would start to rehearse up to six new numbers on the Sunday afternoon and one day, a severe and complex guitar solo came my way and from the moment I saw the dots, I hoped against hope that we would never actually play the thing. True to form, later that night Les called out the new number: my heart sank then and there but, even under pressure, I did play it well and Les made his way across the noisy stage, gave me a thumbs-up sign and bent low to my ear....

"Well done son: I knew that you could do it!"

and he smiled a rare smile as he went away and the lady singer also gave me more than a few glances to add to my 'Feel Good Factor.' This onrush of fame took me high and I played on into the next number with a smile until I collided with an unplayable passage in the music! Everything fell apart and we only just finished the item 'intact' (as they say). Les made his way over the stage once more, striding towards me with a determined look on his face and he bent low to my ear....

"*What I said before, son; I take it all back!*"

That knock-back put me low and to make matters worse, I was sat next to the very desirable singer who seemed so polite, so haughty, so high on a pedestal that I often could not find the words to say when we met. She suddenly frowned and looked at Les and screamed out enough foul language to shame a drunken navvy! We all lived a wild, late-night life then, finishing late and going on later still, never wanting the night to end. It really was the Summer of 69' for all of us.

By the year of 1969, I had become a professional guitarist: I made money only by playing, not dossing, no side-jobs. The nights were long and could be tiring and even dangerous as we have seen and when I started playing the Spanish Guitar, the late hours, drinking, travelling and general carousing played havoc with my intended practice schedule. The <u>real</u> guitar is indeed a very, very difficult instrument to play and in some countries, it is rated above all others. In order to make serious money with my guitar, I had to carve out several free hours each day and devote time to real study. The 'ogre' in my life (hard, physical work) had long vanished but another ogre was eating up the time needed to create a solid Classical repertoire of durable items, so necessary to the trade of the guitar soloist. Incredibly wild parties came and went and it took a long time for a young man in my position to absorb the message that my style had to change both musically and socially. Due to this crazy life style, I rarely took photos and this is something I now regret since a memento or two from that wild time would have been useful here. I did many, many stupid and bizarre things: driving to Oxford just to buy a beer (200km away!), sleeping on a lawn all night, diving into a bath of water fully-clothed, almost falling down a quarry at midnight, sleeping on the floor of a railway station, foolishly dangling our feet out of the back of our Dormobile van as it roared along....I could go on and on into the realms of the truly ridiculous but, perhaps the reader will take my word for it. The What and Why of all of this lies in the time-space we now call The Sixties. Bear in mind too that much of this was done on a small budget and meeting someone with real money only tended to accelerate the madness all round. My absolutely stupid scenarios can wait for another book!

That raw, indelible time left me with one slight regret: not taking the offer from that agent from Liverpool. The fact (and it is fact) that I should have been out there in Germany with the whole Mersey-Manchester combination was a hard nut to swallow particularly since so many of them went on to decent careers (mention only The Beatles, Cilla Black and Freddie Starr). For me to have backed and known ALL of the future pop-idols would have been a coup of the very highest order, a musical Victoria Cross. This mistaken decision on my part should be balanced as this session on the Swinging Sixties draws to a close. Even though The Beatles are now mega-famous, at one time, they were low in the pecking order and their name appeared across the North West playing many of the lowest clubs and haunts for a pittance. One Saturday night long ago, our group played a small gig near Warrington, Cheshire. Like everyone else, I hated dragging my gear out after a job and I slid my Vox amplifier across the dance floor towards the waiting van outside. As I neared the exit doors, a large, red poster caught my eye. The name of our group was emblazoned across in giant, black letters and way, way down at the bottom in very small type, the wording said....

      NEXT SATURDAY....The Beatles (Liverpool).

I like that 'Liverpool bit' don't you?

WAR AND PEACE….

I wanted to join up during my teens, an idea that often appeals to young, energetic people and I was no different to any other. A good friend called Malcolm had been a drummer in the Forces and he warned me that guitar-players and drummers did actually fight: music would not be a cop-out. Any action involving my regiment would also include Neil….ME! By a terrible twist of fate, Malcolm returned to the music profession and was killed in the infamous fire at the Isle of Man Casino. Music, not the Army ended his life.

Many people join up but few are chosen to see action and, if you ask around, still fewer have been in a major battle. The life of a Career-Soldier in peacetime is one thing: when the bullets fly, who actually wants to be there? Some people exaggerate roles too: Bill used to go on and on about his 'tank' (which never saw action) and showed a photo of a 16-ton machine, a baby compared with the huge monsters used in the battles noted here. Some men are either silent or factual about their time spent at war: Harry had fought on D-Day and had taken a bunker <u>single-handed</u>....he was a silent type. Nobody messed with Harry! Jack had fought in Italy and also on the same beaches as Harry where he had shot men stone-dead with his rifle, hating every second of it. I once asked him in 1962, why so few men could be found who had a real frontline tale to tell. His answer was simple: most of his pals were killed in action. They did not survive the heat of battle like the cardboard-heroes of Rambo and such garbage. The Blitzkrieg was so deadly....savage air-attacks and mass shelling followed up by panzers and then flame-throwing troops. To imagine surviving such a blow is to be optimistic to the point of being naive and to even survive without scars would be a rarity. Some of the men I knew did fight the big fight. The Dardanelles, Mons, Tobruk, the Battle of Britain, Cassino, Arnhem, D-Day and also the greatest battles known to mankind, Stalingrad and Kursk. Some we will meet here went behind enemy lines and there are comments from those who were just 'there'....they had no option but to take their place in the inferno of war. Finally in this chapter, I document my own visit to Hell on Earth, the camp at Dachau.

I recall the time when a buff-envelope dropped in my door, reminding me that military service was still a prospect. Seeing such a document with <u>your</u> name and NI number printed on it makes one think, especially if a large military crisis is looming: eighteen is no age to die. Of course, I had music as a distracting career and in a way, it saved me from more misery. For a short while, let these people tell their story, real history told directly to me by the survivors of the most violent century in recorded time.

Back in the fifties, the War seemed so close somehow. Shops had limited supplies, Ration Books abounded and I noticed that my school did not have iron railings and gates; these had long gone to make weapons. At school, my pals jumped about acting the fool playing soldiers as all lads do

37

and Rodney often came in with medals from home. Tom looked at these one day and declared them to be absolute trash....I wanted to know more and so, one day I went home with Tom. Once in his front room, Tom went to a sideboard and from the bottom drawer pulled out a huge red sheet; a flag of immense size....even bigger than his house! A white circle and black swastika adorned the middle and there was more. Tom went back to the drawer and produced a large, red cutlery-style box and this time, a gold swastika gleamed on the lid. Inside, eight amazing crosses shone back at us in the rays of the setting sun; some were Iron Crosses and the neck-ties had diamonds and leaves attached, other crosses had red-enamel with swords. Truly, this was astonishing and I have never seen such a quality display even in a museum. Tom's father had taken them from the corpse of a dead Nazi general whose body had been wrapped in the flag; a suicide with his medals clutched to his chest during the final days of the War. This was a family secret....strange, vivid reminders of those violent days, the laurels of a dead general lying in a little terraced house in Manchester.

    When I was twenty-one, I asked a few pals to come along to a booze-up in town. Old Ted was a great character, an electrician who had after the War worked the entire Canadian-Pacific rail network as a maintenance man....the tales he could tell would have any country-folk singer green with envy and he regularly spoke of Detroit or Chicago or Carson City in the same way that we speak of Leeds or Coventry. He was also in a small way instrumental in the process of my own awareness of the world and real life because he actively promoted the view that the world was open and there for the taking. I knew also that he had faced Rommel's armour in the Desert War and that he chided those who pretended that they too had seen real action. I asked him to go along to the party and he agreed and then fell silent. Tears came into his eyes as he recalled his own 21st birthday out there at El Alamein facing Rommel's troops. That very day, a panzer had blown six of his friends to pieces and he had almost been killed by a Stuka bomber. That had truly been a birthday to remember and he joined in my 'do' as we all guzzled huge quantities of beer and food. What a strange time it must have been for Ted, sat among us with all of his terrible memories.

    In the mid-60's I travelled south and stayed on a farm for the first time in my life. The ruddy-faced farmer gave me the run of the place and I even helped a little with the work....farm work is truly hard and this too gave me more incentive to quit anything laborious and go into music; lazy? Not me. During the long evenings, we all drank the 'Scrumpy'....not pub-cider this but real cider with dirt, flies, straw and all kinds of oddments floating in the brew. The cask was in a barn and one night, I went out to fill a bottle and found a rather scruffy man at the cask filling up a pan with cider. We spoke and I learned that he lived near the farm in a little caravan....he offered me breakfast next day and so I accepted.

As I stepped into the caravan, I noticed a rifle and pistol pinned to the wall and, moving in closer I saw a photo of men in Arab costume alongside a Nazi officer pointing a gun at these Arabs. My new friend laughed out loud; yes, he was one of the Arabs in the picture and the officer was....none other than General Rommel of the Afrika Korps! I sat down to listen as the eggs crackled away on his stove. How had all this come about; who was this strange, new friend and what was Rommel doing in the picture?

It turned out that this guy had been in the Long Range Desert Forces in World War Two. His 'job' was to disrupt supply and fuel lines of enemy units. Basically, he and others had to seek out and destroy tankers and any escort in tow. He spoke fluent Arabic and would dress the part, go along to a market and converse to find out when and where any Nazi units had been seen. Then he would return to his jeep (which had a heavy gun) and set off in pursuit....as I type this and you read it, can you actually feel for these people, can we imagine what went through their minds? One day, he set off to trail a convoy; the gruesome end to his search would mean shooting up the tankers, killing all the escort (with knives if necessary) smashing the radio equipment and leaving fast before the blaze was spotted. Or it would end in his violent death out in the parched desert.

As he searched for tracks and other signs, he drove around a rocky outcrop and came face to face with a Nazi tank! The only option was surrender and soon, a man of high rank appeared and he drew out a Luger pistol and walked menacingly over towards the captives....this was Rommel, The Desert Fox. Rommel apparently stated that he would execute these 'Arabs' on the spot; by not wearing uniforms, they had lost any military rights and would be treated as spies. Relenting, Rommel asked for his photographer to film the group as he held these 'saboteurs' at gunpoint. Later that night, he gave them a meal and the photograph and told them that they would be shipped to Germany to a camp the very next day.

At the end of the War, John (as I came to know him) arrived home in London with few clothes and no money. He went to his old street in town and found the entire place flattened; in one night, the whole street had been blitzed and his family wiped out. John lived as a hermit after this terrible ordeal.

The mid-80's saw me touring in Greece....I travelled over in May and feel sure that it must be the most beautiful time of the year there. My travels started in Salonika where I saw the newly-discovered relics from the tomb of King Philip of Macedonia, the father of Alexander the Great; wall-to-wall gold with gleaming chariots and rubies and even gold laurels and garlands. For me, it was the most astonishing sight I had seen in a museum and I recommend it to any visitor. Leaving the city, I detoured to see many more great sights in the north including Delphi, Olympus and Thermopylae, the battleground of the Spartan heroes and King Leonidas.

On the third day, feeling unwell, I went off to rest in the hotel....the phone disturbed me. A man called Tassos was on the line, sent to assist my travels to Athens....could we meet at 3pm? We met in the hotel bar and he insisted on taking me over to see the concert hall in person because National and Local elections were under way and all buildings had armed guards posted. As we approached the hall, a soldier with a machine-gun stepped out from the shadows and pointed the gun directly at us both. Tassos walked up to him, put his <u>finger</u> in the end of the gun and pushed it to one side! I hesitated at first but then, we went inside, tried the hall and then went back to the hotel where Tassos had ordered English Tea, something he fondly recalled from his time at Oxford. As we chatted away, two large, angry men broke into an argument about politics at the bar; their voices rose quickly to a crescendo and they came to blows without further ado. Tassos excused himself and walked over and pushed the men apart, grabbing the biggest one by the lapels, he proceeded to lecture him....both men suddenly backed away towards the bar, rather like animals slinking into a cave. Tassos returned to us quickly and said he was going to check on the delayed tea!

Our driver sat alongside me throughout this episode and smiled. Apparently, Tassos had been a partisan leader during World War Two and was much respected and no stranger to deadly danger....those men would have been knocked to the ground had they reacted badly. When he returned with the tea, I asked about his story and it seems that he had escaped execution in his village and had joined the Partisans in the mountains, living in deadly peril until the end of the war when he was decorated for his work. Before I left Greece, he invited me to his home where his wife cooked me the most delicious Egyptian meal. He was a tremendous character, someone impossible to forget.

Pieter lived in Holland, a teenager during the War and his brother was in the Resistance. The shortages caused severe queues of almost five hours (each day!) and so Pieter developed a taste for Oriental food where the queues were much shorter; only two or three hours. From Pieter, I got a small taste of what it must have been like to be "Occupied" and as the reader will see, this was a terrifying time for all. One day, he got to the front of the queue when suddenly a large Nazi soldier pushed in front of him. Leaning over the counter, the soldier demanded to be served first, without delay. Totally unfazed by this offensive intrusion and danger, the little Korean man behind the counter took a rather dim view of this and politely asked the soldier to wait. In anger, the soldier pulled out his pistol....the little guy behind the counter anticipated this move and leapt over with a karate-kick, knocking the soldier flying! All hell broke loose and Pieter ran outside with other customers and they hid at the corner to watch the proceedings. The soldier began firing into the shop-counter and soon, the Military Police arrived ready for action. Seeing no-one else around, they assumed that this man had gone berserk and they battered him down with dozens of blows from their batons and he was dragged away: the irony of it all was not lost on Pieter and his companions who, for the first time in the War, found something to smile about.

His brother was a member of the Dutch Resistance and, one Christmas, he risked his life to be at home with the family. As they sat around talking, there came a loud and terrifying hammering at the front door....this could only mean one thing and Pieter was sent to investigate as his brother went into hiding. On opening the door, he was confronted by a man dressed in the dreaded black-uniform of the SS....he bent low to Pieter, his collar-flashes and the skull badges facing the young boy. In the most perfect Dutch, the officer asked him to assemble everyone at once: as Pieter said, it was no use trying to run, guards were posted front and back <u>and</u> the SS used <u>electric</u> cars to avoid making noise as they arrived! All of the family assembled, except the brother, and the officer walked the line, stopping in front of each person, looking directly into the eyes....

"How many persons are in this building?"

That was his question in perfect Dutch. Pieter recalled that families were disappearing regularly in the street where he lived: that night, it could be the end for his family too! Finally, the officer bent low and asked Pieter the same question, a situation sure to raise terror even in the boldest heart. Pieter answered and the officer shouted orders for a search of the building. They did not find his brother who had gone into a secret place beneath the sink, a narrow escape for a brave young man.

Somewhere in my mind I knew that one day I would go beyond that Iron Curtain to the USSR. I had read a good deal about the Eastern Bloc and I also wanted to meet some of the men and women who had fought there in the greatest battles ever known: over twenty-eight MILLION died and many millions were injured. In the city of Volgograd (new name for Stalingrad) I hear that they find human bones almost every day....as this book was finished (June 2001) BBC Online announced that the bodies of 800 Soviet soldiers had just been unearthed, sixty years after the conflict.

One special meeting with someone from those cruel times came on a Russian train journey through the snow, a great way to get to know people and know their country and since some of the journeys are incredibly long (several days!), it is possible to chat and share food and drink with people one would never have met in normal circumstances. The long-haul trains are very good indeed, very comfortable with a cafe-bar, sleepers, etc, etc. Our very long train clanked and groaned as it sped through the night and the Russian darkness seemed to cloak us all as only here and there could one detect a small light in what looked like a vast and unending wilderness. Some passengers walked in the corridor, others were trying to sleep and every now and then, loud laughter would erupt from various compartments as the vodka took effect.I was left alone in my booth apart from another Russian who started to chat away to me causing me to shake my head

"Nyet Russki" I claimed as he offered me more vodka. I told him that I was English and he shook his head then asked if I spoke German; I nodded and so we went on and on in broken German for ages until he suddenly held his glass up and said...."Ich bin Leningrader!" (which I took to mean that he was not just from St. Petersburg but had actually been there in Soviet times). Yes, that was what he meant and this man had lived through the 900-day siege during World War Two. People ate cats and dogs and various disturbing things and some people ate....well, maybe you can guess what they ate. On the small table in our booth was a knife and some bread, cheese, meat, fish and pickles....and Vodka. He took up the bread and cut a small piece off the loaf, one centimetre thick and it just fitted on the palm of my hand....he placed it there solemnly saying....

"Ein tag....ein tag....ein tag...."

Only this each day; nothing else? He nodded. No butter, no spread, no meat, no sugar....nothing else at all? He nodded. And he said that some people boiled shoes, others boiled glue to eat, some boiled their pets and goodness knows what else. I shook his hand and drank a toast with him, a toast in which I hoped that I would never have to suffer anything remotely like this in my life. Recent official statistics claim that perhaps some 2,000,000 people died in the 900-day siege. This man was certainly very lucky to be alive and I felt quite humble as I listened to parts of his story and have no doubt that any reader would have felt the same.

On a bus journey across that bitter Cold War divide, I sat next to a man who had an equally horrific story to tell involving his whole family. His father had been caught up in a purge prior to World War Two and had been sent <u>literally</u> to remote Siberia. As the huge Nazi armoured attack fell on Moscow, his father was called back and put in a Penal Battalion, the most dreaded punishment of all. There at the Front in the ice and snow, he was issued a black cape and ordered with others to walk across <u>active</u> mines towards the enemy line. No-one could refuse or turn back; a squad of Military Security waited in the rear and all who halted or turned were shot dead. Many people (women included) around him were shot and blown to pieces but, by some miracle, he survived and fell into a Nazi trench! He was sent to a concentration camp and during his time there, a wagonload of new prisoners arrived: this new transport by some even greater miracle included his wife <u>and</u> their son, the man sitting on the bus next to me! For this family, more miracles happened because they all survived the War intact and managed to make a good life away from this horror. Reading this, it is worth remembering that most stories of this conflict do not have such a decent ending; the Dirty Dozen and such trash are the stuff of Hollywood, not reality.

And I must not forget those gallant seamen who fought in the Battle of the Atlantic, men like Richard and Arnold who also served in those tremendously dangerous convoys to the Arctic, supplying the USSR across probably the most deadly seas in the world (where incidentally, the submarine Kursk recently sank). I spoke to Richard about it all and he was remarkably cheerful until he mentioned that even a walk up on deck could mean sudden death....men just vanished over the side into the raging storms and to perform bodily functions outside often meant death too. The cold is so intense, so instantaneous and even the eyes can freeze and it is possible to return inside and not realize that your ungloved hand may never work again. Richard also took part in the landings in Italy and his great humour showed through once more. He was helping on a landing-craft and all the soldiers had jumped off leaving the crew and a sergeant-major on board with a tank. The sergeant-major shouted like hell at Richard to get the tank moving and even threatened him; Richard was a seaman and had never driven a tank at any time. Without hesitating a moment longer, he jumped into the machine, somehow started it and drove off....

"I drove it straight into the bloody water, so deep I almost drowned and only just got out alive. They had left the tank on board because they knew that the water was too deep there....my contribution to the war-effort, sinking a tank!"

Nonetheless, whatever happened, we know now how it all turned out and but for people like those mentioned in this chapter, the world could be a very different place today.

Musical events are often followed by a good amount of socializing, chatting, drinking, eating, whatever and it is certainly a good opportunity to make contacts for ongoing events, festivals, etc. After one very successful concert in the East, I sat around talking with some Russian guests and, for the first time, drank some of the amazing Vodka; forget British vodka, it cannot be compared to this spirit really. We drank on and on and I met Vlad and his wife who managed to interpret between us all. As the party ended, we all stood for a final toast, shook hands and Vlad invited me to call for breakfast next day. As he turned away, he walked into <u>and</u> through a table, sending it spinning across the room; he did not flinch! Everyone stared at the event and I wondered if he was made of steel. Next day, my question was answered.

I arrived at his room and his wife showed me in to where Vlad was sitting on the bed. He saluted me by raising a bottle of vodka and stood up and ambled in a most ungainly fashion across the room. On reaching the other bed, he rummaged beneath it and hauled out a crate of vodka....he threw a bottle at me! Catching the bottle, I shook my head and asked why he wanted this so early in the day; his wife continued....

"Vlad was injured in the War in a great tank battle. He lost his legs and the British sent him metal legs which are just like those of a famous airman. We are very grateful...."

Obviously, his new legs were identical to the famous pair of legs made for the air-ace Douglas Bader. I looked across at Vlad as his wild, staring eyes

43

glinted over the upturned bottle. I said the word "Stalingrad?" and they both nodded; Vlad had fought there....the turn of the war according to Churchill and Roosevelt. The name still rings with horror around the globe today and yet, I knew that a colossal battle had followed on. I said the name 'Kursk?' and Vlad stopped drinking and stared at me..."DA!!! DA!!!" (Yes, Yes!) he almost shouted. Hitler's battle-command gives some indication of the nightmare...

'Soldiers! Today you set out on a great slaughter, the outcome of which could well decide the War...your victory at Kursk must be a blazing torch to the world!'

General Hoth's tanks smashed into the Soviet trenches and mercilessly ground up the poor soldiers defending, soldiers went mad with the shellfire and the sky darkened with the sheer volume of aircraft. This was what the BBC called The Mother of All Battles and it ruined an area as large as Wales...the debris and bodies would have filled up the circle made by the new London M25 Motorway.

I looked again at Vlad's metal legs and noticed for the first time rivet-lines showing through the cloth. His wife said that the trousers only lasted three months or so...I grabbed the beaker of vodka and gulped it down. I almost choked and my eyes watered as Vlad let out a huge laugh, the one time I saw him smile. That time with Vlad was the Summer of 1983, exactly 40 years since what has become known as The Death Ride of The Panzers and no-one knows exactly how many lives this monster-battle cost. Both Hitler and Stalin hid the true figures. Vlad's lot must have been like so many millions out there, the terrifying fight for Stalingrad followed up with the most enormous clash of arms at Kursk, the battle that made Adolf Hitler's stomach turn over. What can one say in the presence of such people?

I doubt if I could have arranged these meetings even if I had tried. So many times Fate has put such things in my path, even at one time placing a concert within reach of Dachau Concentration Camp. On a harsh winter day, I stood in the former SS Office and silently watched three women crying and shrieking at a life-size photograph. On the floor in front of them I saw a pool of tears and the eldest woman fell down, screamed and put her hands onto the photo as her friends prayed in Polish. Her long-dead relative stared back at us all across the silent void of 50 years...never, never have I felt such a deep inner despair, not even in my worst times.

When I returned to the UK, I met Emile, an old musician and told him of the trip; his eyes glistened with tears. He had been there as a prisoner! He rolled his sleeve back to the astonishment of the hotel staff and pointed to his number on his arm. His violin had saved him, gaining him rest and food during his 300 days in the camp, days marked by beatings, and attacks by huge dogs and he spoke of the *Strafappell* where everyone stood a night and half a day outside if someone tried to escape.

All of these people mentioned in this chapter told me so much more, some of it so incredibly violent and ghastly but, I will close now this period in my life knowing that perhaps the reader feels as I do...that we are really very lucky indeed to have safety and comfort around us.

At the Military Museum in Moscow, I decided to take a closer look at a real battle-tank, a T-34 Soviet model, the best of all tanks according to Hitler's generals. This actual machine fought at Stalingrad (see photo) a fight which used up explosives equal to 100 Atomic Bombs. As I stepped up onto the tracks of this aged colossus, I had to grip the handrails and pull myself up, just like those men and women who rode these into battle, clinging on for dear life as fire and shells swept the frontline. Then they jumped off into live minefields: the Red Army did not clear mines. Soldiers themselves did that risking death with every step. Nor could they halt or delay action; Military Police monitored the whole event and anyone who did not comply with Stalin's commands was shot dead. Sometimes, we all feel brave but, in reality, we will never, ever have to face anything like this. A film has just been made of the Stalingrad battle called Enemy at The Gates.

What does it all amount to? For one thing, Conscription ended during my teens and young people had a choice: to go into The Forces or not. That huge war had changed Europe and the World. Hitler's war had cost him his life and the lives of fifty-six million others and it had led directly to a Cold War....a strange war in which many (including myself) made much money as we churned out guns and rockets for the war to come, the Third World War. Personally, I had big musical plans and the Army did not fit in with such plans. Additionally, I had met real heroes who had a ghastly tale to tell, enough to put anyone off a military career. Perhaps after reading this chapter we should all be glad that we were never part of the Legion of The Doomed....forced to walk towards violent death in −35° Centigrade, guns in front and behind, mines under our feet as we play out our small part in the most savage conflict ever known. Trouble? Maybe we don't even know the half of it.

45

MUSICIANS IN THE EAST, 1983.
From the left; Gareth Walters (BBC Producer), Guerra (guitarist), Romanillos (guitar-maker) and guitarists Cotsiolis, Käppel, Artzt, Smith, Galbraith (at rear). Then Vlad (with cap) and Acosta. Grondona kneeling at front.
Courtesy, Zbigniew Dubiella.

MOSCOW MILITARY MUSEUM.
A serious T-34 tank from the Battle of Stalingrad. Did you know that a woman paid for a tank with her savings and drove it into a battle? Another woman lost NINE sons! U2 Spy Planes and incredible relics at this great museum.   Courtesy, Svetlana Lukianova

HAVE YOU ANYTHING TO DECLARE?

Crossing borders: no problem to most travellers although one can get hassle from unexpected quarters sometimes. Passing over the French border once, the guard took one look at my guitar strapped to the roof and pointed and raised his head in that questioning way only the French seem able to do. I pointed to myself and, in an act of great internationalism, I said the French word "Orchestre" (meaning Orchestra). Taking me at my word, the official ordered us all out of the car, took all of the luggage out, had the car and engine inspected, mirrors underneath and <u>still</u> after all of that, he looked at me and shrugged his shoulders. He wanted to know....where WAS the Orchestra, where were the instruments? I decided to shut up and wait for someone with a decent command of the lingo and we wasted one hour of time, not to mention the unloading and re-loading in the hot sun. My colleagues thought little of my pathetic attempts at ANY language from then on and I was always the last to be consulted in any dispute about signs, notices or orders.

Officially, people are supposed to take care of you: it says so in your passport, if you don't believe me, go and look! And they should also take care of your things too. Once, I changed aircraft at Atlanta, Georgia, USA and I had sent my guitar through as a transfer, not by hand. Sitting on the jet, I noticed a guitar-shaped case like mine, rocking on top of a pile of luggage as the little wagon pottered to and fro between aircraft. The guitar fell off; it <u>was</u> my case, and a man with a large grappling hook took hold through the handle and hurled this onto the case elevator-belt! Later, I inspected the case and could not even find a mark! Often, such treatment will wreck the whole thing, inside and out. In Italy, my homeward flight was much delayed and I sat sadly in the terminal, just able to view the gate on the ground. Sure enough, my guitar case was out there in the baking sun, one of the hottest days anyone could recall! Hours went by and I tried to retrieve it to no avail. By the time I checked it out in Manchester, the combined weather-changes had produced loads of water around the wood and for days, I worried about the final outcome. Again, such an event did no real damage.

Travelling behind the Iron Curtain always gave problems, more especially because of the instruments. Guards often wanted to confiscate the guitar, maybe to keep themselves. On one trip, the guard brought his friend into the room with a machine-gun as he searched the case and then demanded proof of ownership. This is usually shown by an insurance paper (which I had forgotten). When I confessed this to him he ranted....

"Then I will take it from you now! You will get a receipt and can collect it when you return!"

Somehow, I didn't believe him and I stood there as both men stared back, waiting for my next move. I recalled the official invitation, which was a most impressive document, with black italic writing and a huge red lion printed on it with a wax seal. I showed it to him and he looked amazed and, pointing to the phone number on top, I asked him to phone up and allow me to complain about him! His eyes blazed at me and he fumed for a while. Suddenly, he relented and let me go in....with my guitar!

Travelling from one foreign country on to another presents very special problems as I found out when I went from the USA into Canada. Landing in Seattle, I was almost sleepless there! My guitar-pals in Vancouver had assumed that I would fly in direct days later: I had decided to cross by coach on the Pacific border at midnight. Panic phone-calls revealed that I did not have an entry permit until later in the week and I was told to take pot-luck and raced out of the phone-booth and onto the already-moving coach. The bus rumbled on into the night, deep forests lined our route and, after what seemed like an age, we pulled into a depot: The Pacific Border Post. A huge Ranger stepped on the coach and he walked the floor with menace, looking in turn at each of the seven people on board and asking questions. He approached me sitting way back....

"That yer geetar, Boy?"

he drawled in an almost John Wayne style. I nodded and he ordered me off the coach into the dark night and told me to go into the station; Pronto! He clomped in after waving the bus off and went behind his desk, over six feet high and as broad....he opened up on me.

"Ya think yer gonna play that there geetar in Canada, Boy?"

I told him of the original plan and he smiled a sarcastic smile telling me that I would have to leave back to Seattle! I protested and he then revealed an ace in the pack....

"Well boy; ya can sleep right there on the floor in the entrance OR, if ya give me trouble, ya can sleep in that there cell!"

So saying, he pointed back over his shoulder to a barred-room out back. I asked for a line to Immigration and he said they were closed. Using my final change, I called Vancouver, I got through to my pals who came down hot-foot with various papers and forms; the Ranger smiled....

"Weel boy....looks like yer ok fer travel. See y'all!"

Going back, I had the reverse problem. The Customs man did <u>not</u> believe that I was a guitarist and so I told him that the only way to settle it was for me to actually play something for him! There, in the queue with thronging travellers all around, I grabbed my guitar and, just as I was about to kick off, he stopped me: he had an idea....

"Ya say yer a geetar player? OK, then let me see those nails!"

I showed him my long right-hand nails and he smiled and pushed me through.

Flying in Germany once, I came across the nightmare of ALL stewards who was arguing with everyone, not just me. As he clocked my guitar, he asked if I had paid for it, telling me as he did so that Lufthansa would make a charge for hand luggage....£250 in our money! I knew that it would fall on expenses on that trip and so I paid and when I got on the aircraft, only twelve seats were taken! I had to officially strap my guitar into a seat! Due to this and the over payment, I decided to be cheeky and I told the nice lady stewardess what had happened and I then asked for a meal for my guitar! She looked shocked and laughed but brought me another tray! On landing, I summoned an angry pose and went to the desk, moaning and moaning about the empty seats: I got my money back too!

Heading from Salonika to London, we sat early one beautiful morning as the pink sunlight shot across the East. It was already hot and very dusty, the humid air in the aircraft was not moving at all. Our flight time had long expired and I saw outside signs of activity: a fire engine and some police wagons. Earlier that week, a terrorist bomb had hit Frankfurt Airport and many were killed. Announcements came over the intercom....

"Will all passengers have their boarding-passes and tickets ready quickly please?"

Worried-looking stewardesses toured the plane and then: silence. Much later, the Captain came on to say....

"I am afraid that we have a problem. We have passes cleared for 150 persons but only 149 are on this flight: I don't want to worry you but..."

I couldn't hear the rest of his message. People began to talk loud. Some wailed out, others just looked around, scared. The Captain came on once more with a terse and doom-laden message....

"Please pay close attention to your nearest Exit Door and be ready to use it if necessary....Unfasten your seatbelts!"

I was worried by this time and I looked across to a lady and told her in jest really in jest! When I told her the reason (she was old and deaf) she panicked and almost cried. We waited for an age or so it seemed and then, rather than get us all off, they came once more to do a headcount! All at once the mystery was clear. A woman with a small child had set the child down on spare seats under a heap of blankets and of course, in the head and ticket count, he was not spotted. Once again they counted as the child woke up screaming and the doors began to close. The aircraft shot away into the clear sky at long last....and I drank and drank for England!

Leaving Moscow after a truly memorable time, I encountered The Law again. As we sped along those massive avenues across the city, traffic soon dropped to a crawl and then stopped dead. The French President was in town and all roads on his route were simply closed off. I sat as I have done so many, many times watching those minutes tick by as the whole citadel seemed locked in a vice-like grip as nothing moved for almost an hour. Arriving at Departures we hurried along and I rushed changing money and filling forms and then said my goodbyes, making for Security Clearance. The officer seemed in no particular rush at all and when he scanned my papers, he started asking questions, questions, questions.

Something in my papers was not correct and he told me that I could not leave Russia. As I protested a VERY large guard un-strapped his Kalashnikov and walked across to me, his heavy boots almost clanking on the marbled floor. His annoyance was visible and he seemed to be saying....

"What is all this? Is my pal in trouble? I'LL SORT IT OUT!"

As they both looked at my cases and papers it was decided that I should go back out of the terminal and do all checks again; everything had to be rechecked/rewritten and, eventually I arrived back at the same officer's desk. The officer saw my new papers, cleared them and pointed me through the barriers. As I ran for the ticket desk, a stewardess ran out to meet me....

"No, no, you cannot go there. It is closed....no flight for you!"

It was pointless; my friends returned but no way would they let me onto the flight and so I waited for a night flight to Amsterdam and slept on Schipol floor as I waited for a connection to Manchester. I arrived back home at 11am and went to bed until 3pm: I had a rehearsal at 5pm for a night concert with the superb soprano Lorna Rushton.

In the 1980's, I was booked for a great tour with the City of Birmingham Symphony Orchestra under their star conductor Simon Rattle. We made a start in Birmingham with a BBC concert then flew to Holland, the CSSR, Austria and Germany for two weeks, all paid for with good salaries to boot. One concert called for us to cross the land border into the CSSR, our 24-hour visas draining away we waited in the hot sun as guards took our passports....on each side for miles signs....

ACHTUNG!!!   MINEN!!!   ACHTUNG!!!   MINEN!!!

Earlier, we had stopped at the home of the great Haydn and had also seen the place where he made his reputation (Esterhazy Palace) from the coach....but, right now the huge minefields and the towers shimmered in the heat-haze as we all waited, no food, no drinks and large boards with the mine-warnings displayed a skull, watching us with an evil smile. I sat the hours away with a fascinating man with more than a tale to tell of his father, who had fought in those deadly battles before Moscow in the War, and almost too late, we sped into the city to set up. Intent on finding food and drink, I wandered into a hotel doorway; a man stopped me....

"You are American? Yes, you are OR maybe you are English? Then you need money; our money. Get it from me now....here, here. Take some."

I looked up at the silent security cameras: the penalty then for illegal money changing was anything up to 14 years in prison! I pushed past him into the foyer, found the restaurant, tried to order in German and got a totally different meal than I had expected! Our concert hall was 'jam-packed' and Simon Rattle stepped on stage, raised his baton and looked puzzled....members of the orchestra were all pointing up at a balcony out in the crowd. A microphone on a silver stand was peeping over the edge: a hubbub followed during which it was announced that:

"RECORDING OF THESE CONCERTS IS NOT PERMITTED!"

The microphone sheepishly vanished and we set out to play. My part in the proceedings ended early and I wandered alone into the dark, dismal streets, the cobbles and tramlines snaking away into a rather mysterious 'Third-Man' scenario. On I wandered until the light and sounds of a tavern beckoned on my left. Striding in, bowtie and tail suit still intact, I stopped the whole place dead and stood at the bar. A waitress spoke to me in German and I showed her the money and asked for beer. She laughed and hauled up a case of 24 bottles! I bought it and went quickly away with my treasure, a few of the people in there seemed rather dodgy to say the least. Staggering back into the stage door, Simon saw me as he ran offstage and asked about the beer.

"Save one for me later!"

he shouted as he ran back for an encore. At midnight, we sat in the evil minefields as our visas expired, drinking beer as the ever-watchful guards prowled around the coach with their dogs and machine-guns. Soon, we were back at the Sauerhof in Baden-Baden and I was lucky enough to stay in a room once occupied by the great Beethoven.

On the same trip but on another subject, we were joined later by the distinguished pianist Peter Donahoe whose wife Elaine was playing in the main orchestra. In one city, we could not find decent food and I made comment that we would have to find a burger-joint. At this idea, Peter groaned and in mock-misery declared....

"No, No....Don't say that Neil!"

Later that night, I had found a hamburger place and I sat alone as the door opened furtively and in walked Peter and his wife, trying to look casual. I waited in the shadows as they went up to the order girl and just as they put in their order, I emerged shouting....

"Well! Well! Now who have we got here then?"

We all collapsed in laughter, the whole event being lost on the puzzled ladies behind the counter.

In California, I hoped to travel into Mexico and I set off with Martin heading for the border. We stopped at a nice bar and soon forgot about the 'Border' idea as we drank and ate the hours away. Heading back into L.A. the car suddenly vaulted forwards, revving and spluttering along in the fast lane. The traffic line to our side would not let us in and we had no alternative but to bump onto the central reservation and go onwards until a clear exit showed up. Eventually, we got across the highway and off the ramp, stopping at some lights near to a magazine store. Several burly, violent-looking characters eyed our car and Martin sent me out to the store to get change to phone the Triple-A (America's A.A.). I didn't know it but the district was called Watts, an area known for trouble and I was out walking alone. Entering the store, the guy behind the counter eyed me suspiciously and, as I reached into my right pocket for some dollars he reached under the counter and pulled out a machine-gun! Sticking it into my chest, he demanded to know what the 'game' was. I explained what I wanted and he put the gun down....

"Well feller, you were mighty lucky there. Don't you ever reach in that pocket here unless you draw a gun, ok? You just put your dough in your back pocket."

He smiled, shaking his head and then he looked across to the car....

"That your car there boy? (I nodded). You leave that there boy and your wheels will go by midnight and the whole car will be a cinder by mornin'....bet your life!"

Already, the bad-guys had got closer to our car but luckily, Martin had seen a garage sign just over the lights and we pushed the car over and left it until next day. I never did get South of The Border but at least I made it back to Glendale by taxi and without any bullet holes.

In Germany in 1987, I went to that old symbol of division, The Berlin Wall. In dark winter, the sombre setting seemed a harsh throwback to 1945 as the Brandenburg Gate stood gaunt against the sky and The Reichstag still showed shell and bullet-marks from that last, terrible battle. And up the road in the mist was a Soviet T-34 tank, its exits welded shut sealing the bodies of those brave soldiers inside: a memorial to it all. I walked up onto a podium built to give a view of the 'other' side and, on seeing my guitar, quite a few guards came out of the Control Post. They signalled for me to play a little guitar for them and so I held up the case as they photographed away: only later did someone tell me that I had been lucky not to get a shot aimed my way!

These problems are not exclusively international, since often one can experience quite awesome trouble, moving within the same country. On a trip north in Russia, I took all documents and contracts with me on leaving Moscow and, after five days, I was summoned to an office by a very serious-looking secretary. She announced that I had moved without special permission and that the Police and KGB wanted to know my whereabouts. Two KGB men had arrived to speak with me and to confiscate my passport and documents and it was only after much explanation that everything was returned to me three days later. Such things may seem like nothing special when told in this way but of course, when you are a long way from home and without help or guidance, events have a more worrying nature and some offences abroad can attract extremely high sentences in appalling conditions, without parole.

At one time, my late-wife Carol ran an antique shop and often, amazing items would appear for sale at auction. At a viewing, she called me over to a small, scruffy box of music and asked...."Is there a composer called Byrd, spelt B-Y-R-D?" I nodded and she pointed to nothing less than a manuscript near some old pop-copies and we went home for my chequebook. On returning at night, we found to our dismay that a huge reserve price had been put on the box; six months later in The Times, a publisher announced his find. He got there first and with more money. We also came across a set of Pot-Heads....seven film-stars heads made life-size and one was of the great Chaplin. I told my friend Alice in America about this find and she bought the head; I had to transport it to New York. On arrival at Customs, I dragged in a large, sinister bag carefully packed and the officer asked me directly what was in the bag....I told him: "A Head!" He almost jumped in the air and shouted over a gang of his colleagues who opened the top carefully, parting the bubble-wrap and screaming with laughter as they lifted out the head of Charlie Chaplin!

Even in The Land of The Free, crossing County Lines and State Lines can cause a few problems, especially if you bend the rules! Motoring up from New York to Connecticut, I seemed to be making rather good time. My co-driver was the American guitarist Alice Artzt and we had left the city early that day due to a massive bridge-fault, which almost closed the city roads down. Shortly after crossing the State Line, I became aware of a loud, humming noise in the car, a low pitched whirring sound. I switched a few dials but nothing seemed wrong when suddenly, a large shadow appeared over our car, hovering above.....Alice woke up and looked quickly at the speedometer in the car....oh boy! The Police chopper hailed down to us and I slowed down and almost at once, a State Trooper drove alongside running parallel to our vehicle. He shouted over to ask me where the fire was as we both drifted along, the chopper soared away out of sight. I shouted back to say that I was sorry; this caused him to shout back across the gap....

"You're English, right? Then just forget it man!"

Never has that journey been completed so fast legally by any other car!

Sometimes, due to the incredible hassle, I wonder why I get into all of this, but then, it is not music-making that actually causes the problems. Most pro-players will have a horror story or two in repertoire I can bet. Once I drove up to Scotland for a concert only to find that the concert was actually on the twelfth; of the FOLLOWING month! Anything to declare? Well, I guess I'm a crazy guitarist!

WITH MICHAEL BERKELEY AND JOHN TURNER.

WITH LEO BROUWER (Blues at 3am!)

WITH JOHN DUARTE (talking music).

WITH THOMAS PITFIELD AND JOHN TURNER IN APRIL 1981.
Thomas was a superb composer, writer and artist and an expert on birdsong.
His wife Alice was actually caught up in the Russian Revolution in 1917.

WITH JULIAN B. COCO IN HOLLAND, 1979.
Julian 'jamming along' with me in Breda, a great bassist and composer/guitarist
Photo, Els Breukers.

WITH STEPAN RAK
(playing his music).

TRAINS, BOATS, PLANES....
AND TANKS?

Travel, as someone once said, does broaden the mind. It can also be dangerous too and many great artists have fallen victim to real accidents....events which could in no way be predicted. Granados the pianist was world-famous a century ago and he journeyed to the USA along with his wife to play and to premiere his opera before the President. His return was delayed and the ship he eventually did take was torpedoed by a submarine; he and his wife both died. More recently, one can cite the examples of Buddy Holly and Eddie Cochran, the great rock singers. The world is a big place whatever mode of transport you choose and finally getting to that destination can involve the traveller in all kinds of problems: as we will see in this chapter.

A journey can bring excitement into one's life and yet, as a child, I was rather stay-at-home partly due to a queasy stomach which thankfully vanished in later years. My travels up to 1970 were more often than not confined to the view out of a group-van window as the vehicle strained to carry us on to fame and fortune. In the early sixties, we did all borrow a car to make the long journey from Manchester to Great Yarmouth and the Ford Popular seemed reasonable enough to me as it struggled over The Pennines and into Sheffield. The glow of the city furnaces is one sight I will never forget. Huge blasts of fire, lighting up the night sky and the heat, down amongst it all was quite incredible. We moved on over to the A1, a 'big' road in those days and it was so quiet at 3am that we all had an impromptu football match on the surface! This only ceased when little lights appeared a long way off as cars trundled along at a snail's pace.

On we rumbled across strange, low fields quite unlike my own area and soon we emerged onto some vast, open plain, the road only marked by two painted lines reaching out into the blackness. A sign told us to HALT and WAIT. Ages went by and Dave lost his patience, the vote in the car being unanimous in favour of going ahead. We set off, following the white lines and to my right, I saw a faint glow, a greenish-light moving fast to the side. The glow began to move faster than before, vibrating as it did so, looming....suddenly it emerged from the darkness: a giant Vulcan V-Bomber taking off over our heads! The roar was immense and the car shook almost to pieces: I saw the pilot shaking his fist at us as he went overhead! Then the red-white hot exhaust hit back at us as the plane soared upwards and vanished into the depths of night. The journey continued until we were met by Military Police, all waiting on the far side of the airstrip; this was RAF Waddington and we were in trouble. After much explaining and serious banter, we were allowed off, our cameras had been examined since the V-Bombers were part of the frontline defence systems against the Eastern Bloc at the time.

By late morning, we were in Great Yarmouth. We stayed exactly one day, got drunk and then travelled back to Blackpool through the whole day, taking care to stop at Waddington this time!

Beyond 1970, I started to make headway as a guitar soloist and this placed on me more responsibility for transport, the pain of musicians. I was booked for a last minute job near to Portsmouth and, due to a rail dispute, I opted to go by car....a BAD move! I played the ever-popular Concierto de Aranjuez that night and it was very nearly the last night I ever played anything. Finishing the work at around 9pm, I figured that I could make it to the North before tiredness hit me and so, with a nice handshake and farewell to the orchestra, I set off into the freezing night on my journey; a journey which ended in terror. The silver-disc of a full moon floated to my right as the miles went by, the bitter frost making the landscape deathly-pale, almost ghostly by normal standards. Heading for Reading then Oxford, I made good time until some traffic signals stopped me and stayed on red....for ages. The lights were obviously out of action and I was just about to move off cautiously when lights appeared behind me, moving fast; VERY fast! The car smashed into the rear of my own as I waited inside, secure in my seatbelt. I opened my door and stepped into the swirling mist, turning back towards the other vehicle. My exhaust was down, the bumper broken, one light hanging lose: I walked up to the driver's door and stood against his car. Looking through the glass, I saw his eyes, staring wildly at me and I stepped back; that action saved my life. I turned and pointed to the damage on my car and, as I did so, I heard his window drop. Turning back, I saw a carving-knife heading towards my face!!!! I ran back to my car, locked the door and....the car would not fire! The man behind backed off and bumped me again, almost as if to push me across the lights. He backed off again then drove alongside me, brandishing the knife as he did so! Like a flash, he was gone and I had presence of mind to take his number which I muttered to myself, over and over as I fumbled with the smashed exhaust and light.

Not long after, sirens wailed and strobe-lights flooded the sky. Two cars dashed past me and a third car halted nearby. The officer asked what had happened; he rushed back to his car and took up the microphone....

"He still has the knife: pass on the message!"

Calmly taking a clipboard out of his car, he asked me to describe the whole incident. Fortunately, I had my heavy Canadian winter coat on as we stood motionless for ages talking in the bitter night-fog. I finished off and he raised his eyebrows saying....

"Well Mr Smith, you have had a lucky escape: he has already killed three people. You could have been Number Four!"

I slid against my car, propping myself up against the metal body as the officer went on....

"You may find that you will suffer shock soon. If I were you, I would go now to a hotel and lock your car."

Somehow, I decided not to be deterred by all of this and I took out some spare guitar strings and lashed up the exhaust at the broken strap-point and found the missing screw to hold the light in place. The car started and soon, I was en-route again; slowly. Beyond Oxford, I began to feel quite ill and tired and I pulled into a lay-by and fell into a deep sleep. Waking up in the early hours, I set off again and had a good run home, arriving in after 7am. My wife turned as I came into the bedroom and asked what had happened. I told her....

"Don't ask....I'll tell you later."

Trains are my favourite form of transport, without a doubt. some are almost a fantasy ride like, for example, the day journey from Oslo to Bergen where for hours on end, you travel through what can only be described as a Winter Wonderland. Some Russian trains are superb too, German trains are so incredibly efficient and on time, American trains cope with distance at two levels; pay more and you should get there on time, pay less and....well. Playing in Holland near to Christmas, I was in a hurry to get home to my family. I dashed around Schipol then Heathrow and it seemed as if I had a chance to make it to Euston to take the express northwards. On the exact minute, I arrived at Euston; the red tailights of my train rolled away into the night, leaving me alone and rather sad as I contemplated the long, boring hours of waiting to come. This saved my life. I was extremely hungry and planned to upgrade my travel and eat in the Diner Car on the train. Instead, I had to make do with a humble burger and Coke as I sat in the buffet. Time went by and soon, I heard commotion out on the station foyer. People were calling in the buffet with worried expressions on their faces; I went out to see what was going on. All of the Arrival Boards went blank and an announcement was made....

"Due to a serious crash near Stafford, there will be no trains to the North-West and Scotland until further notice."

I found an inspector and heard that the train I had intended to catch had been hit by another train; the Dining Car had been written off and a number of passengers were dead! I spent the rest of the night moving via Kings Cross up to Leeds and across to Manchester next morning, a very tedious, annoying journey....but at least I was alive.

On my first trip to Holland, I tried the boat-journey to the Hook of Holland. Since I was intending to make a broadcast on the next evening for Radio Hilversum, I needed rest and some peace. No such luck. My place on board happened to be next to a Soul-Band who drummed and sang the night away, in and out of rooms, on deck, in bars....everywhere in fact. In the end, I decided to get up and join in, watching the cold dawn as the boat pulled into the quay. Never again go sea (I thought) and that is how it has stayed.

Even though people say that air travel is safe, I have my doubts; things DO go wrong, don't they? I have missed four flights during my career:

this is not like missing a train, believe me! In the early 80's, I planned a tour in Norway, got to Heathrow and was told to check-in with SAS. We went through all formalities, stepped onto the jet and took off. As we soared upwards, the reassuring voice of the captain glided over the intercom....

"Welcome aboard this SAS flight to Copenhagen, our flight...."

I jumped in my seat; I was heading for Bergen!!! Quickly, I rang the Steward and a lady came along with an angry expression....

"Please don't press that when we are taking off!"

I showed her my ticket and she too let out a gasp, shook her head and ran up to the main cabin. Of course, nothing could be done, we went on to Denmark and I transferred to yet another flight, my third that day. In 1980, I flew to Zurich as a guest of Takamine, the Japanese guitar experts and I must say, I was treated like royalty (as they say here). Limosines ran me here and there, 5-star comfort, a concert to play, a class and a guitar demo with three guitars; one for Paco de Lucia, one for Bert Jansch and another for me, a gift from Takamine. After five days, I went back to the hotel to collect my bags; the taxi was late....VERY late. Eventually, he came and we rushed to the airport only to see my BA flight to London soar over our heads! The driver mumbled an apology but I got him to the BA desk and they phoned his firm at once and they were charged £250 for a new ticket, a very expensive taxi ride!

On one flight to Norway, I sat with men from an oil-platform unit who were going back to work. As I began my tour in Bergen, news came in that their platform had caught fire: many were killed in the explosion. I still recall them laughing at the idea of a guitarist making money from 'music' as I seemed equally astonished at them making money, drilling into water.

Norway featured in my life for a good while and I recall flying out in deep winter and the captain came on air with news...

"We may divert to Oslo today due to bad weather. More information will come later."

Soon, the flight-time had expired and the captain spoke again....

"We may try landing in Bergen: we will see."

The word 'Try' worried me and as we went down, I could just see the Control Tower lights glimmering to the side. We touched down; no sound or sensation of impact as we skidded onwards. Suddenly, the aircraft revolved and the nose pointed at the Control Tower!!! We lunged forwards and I pulled up my seat-strap tight as the woman across from me counted rosary beads and clasped her hands! Very, very slowly, the jet returned to a normal posture and the captain himself seemed relieved as he said....

"Welcome to Bergen; we hope that you had a nice flight!"

That night, I decided to take up serious drinking for a while!

In 1987, the BBC asked me to play in Belfast, or to be more precise, to record a programme there. I alone selected the date which turned out to be the centre-point of the Marching Season: 86 bands were due on the streets that very day. I landed and a great character of a taxi-driver asked me....

"What brings you here on a day like this?"

I told him of my BBC job and he said that he had to at least try the direct-city route to studio since that was the standard fare. We set off, into the unknown. Many roads were blocked as we drove past long, regular terraces pointing into the city centre. One road seemed clear and we went onward until the driver pressed his brakes. We halted, the Lada engine spinning noisily as we waited, looking ahead. Over 100 yards away, two telegraph poles had been placed across the road, making a diagonal 'X' between the houses. He spoke....

"I don't like this....I don't like it one bit! I had one taxi burnt out you know....we should go back!"

I agreed with him but, just then, a small boy in a balaclava ran out from one house and threw a bottle at the barrier: the cross-poles erupted in flames! The wheels of our taxi screamed as we reversed quickly away, onto another road! The BBC building was surrounded by barbed-wire then, this being the limit for any vehicle during these disturbances and, with a hearty farewell, the taxi-driver directed me towards the main entrance. I walked the barbed wire until I found a break and, carrying my guitar and a bag, I strolled through....a bad move. As I walked across the open square, a voice boomed out and shattered the silence...."HALT!" I walked on, not thinking that the order applied to me! Soon, another voice rang out....

"BRITISH ARMY....HALT! DROP THE CASES!"

I turned and saw to my horror a soldier aiming a rifle at me from the corner of a building: he waved his rifle, signalling me to put the cases down and I stood absolutely still. An armoured car came across the precinct and stopped in front of me, the top opened and a young man popped out....

"Open the cases now, quickly!"

I did just that and he reported the guitar and clothes, etc. I closed the cases and went on into the BBC: imagine recording after this, I thought! I did record, with the BBC Ulster Orchestra and added some solos. There's no business like show business!

This may seem dangerous but in ordinary, daily travel, I have been exposed to life-threatening situations. En-route to London on an Inter-City, we passed under a bridge at speed and, without warning, a violent crash ran along the top of the carriage roof. The power lines came down carrying 25,000 volts and sparked and flashed as the express roared onwards. The lady opposite me seemed to enjoy this firework display but, when a cable smashed against the window, we both realized that we could easily be cut in two! The cables whipped the side of the train and gradually, the whole thing stopped and we stayed for ages like this, waiting on the track. Eventually, we were dragged away; some boys had thrown a bicycle onto the overhead lines and this had tangled everything up! On one occasion, I played Queen Elizabeth Hall in London and, due to other commitments, I needed to travel back on the last train. Arriving at a Northern Line station, I waited patiently on the empty platform. Not a sound came to my ears until two very sinister-looking guys walked out from around a pillar and looked menacingly at me and my guitar! I know when people mean business and I can say that they were trouble for me. A train was heading in, I could feel the air-wave but, would it be in time: or maybe I needed to run back upstairs???? This ran through my head as they both sidled up the platform and the train rushed out of the tunnel! I got on the train: an empty coach and THEY got into the same coach! Thinking hard, I recalled a film with Charles Bronson in where he jumped out as the doors closed; I measured the distance and waited, the doors hissed and I ran off, pulling my gear behind!!! The two thugs sneered as the train rumbled out of the station and seemed to be muttering....

" *He got away man....HE GOT AWAY!!!!*"

More than once I went across from Bergen to Oslo on what I called the Train in The Sky, an amazing journey which rises thousands of feet through pleasant valleys with roaring streams and such sparkling waterfalls and on into forests and glades as travellers sit and watch the spectacle go by in luxury. Eventually, the train makes it onto a vast, frozen plateau with permanent ice-cover, the sun becoming blinding as ice crystals shoot light across the wilderness. There, the engine halts and passengers can walk around a little but, the temperature is cold enough to kill. As the mountains climb up on each side, the rails enter a long, snake-like tunnel which keeps them free in all-weather. I recall sitting in the Dining Car eating steak and drinking lager as this hostile vision sailed by. Once over the snowfield, I saw the sun sinking in the West and the downhill to Oslo looked inviting until I saw the sheer drops on each side of the rails and shut my eyes, trying not to think of brake-failure!

In the pink afterglow, we were met at the station by a rep from the music society there and we chatted and lugged our cases towards the exit. Suddenly, the rep pointed at a poster with my name on showing the concert details and, with horror, I saw the word 'FRIDAY' printed. My itinerary showed Stockholm on Friday, NOT Oslo! I showed my rail tickets dated for Stockholm and frantic phone calls and faxes were made to alter the date to Wednesday, my original schedule; no luck, it did not work and much money was lost all round. Wednesday night saw us sitting in front of a bistro, drinking many lagers until the sun vanished as we bemoaned our losses and saw a man jumping from a crane (Bungee) towards the water in the fjord. I actually felt like jumping WITHOUT the cord.

In the Seventies, I played often in Birmingham and was delayed many, many times at that (sorry!) most horrible station, New Street. One dark, very cold winter's night, I stood waiting for a last express as the 'happy' announcer chimed out....

"Due to frozen points near Bristol, the 23-45 Manchester train will be TWO HOURS late. We apologize for this delay."

The Buffet had just closed, people raided their pockets for change for the drinks-food machines as the cruel, freezing, fog crept into the oppressive underworld. At 2.30am, a small light flickered out in the mist and ever so slowly, a grime-covered train rolled in; heaters NOT working! Our miserable entourage eventually shuffled past commuters in Piccadilly, haggard, hungry, angry and cold as we attempted to make a mass-raid on the fast-food desks. Still, this was not as disturbing as a Birmingham journey when football fans went berserk and wrecked the Buffet Car. The waiter ran out, locked the door and stood near me as we heard the destruction beyond. As we pulled into Crewe, a mass of big Police dogs snarled their way into the Buffet and at once, a horde of people shuffled off. Another delay for me....Have Guitar, Will Travel....if you can actually get there!

Although many strange events have happened to me in the UK, I always somehow felt that even stranger things would happen abroad, especially in the East: I was not to be disappointed. One summer, I went to the marvellous city of Prague and it was at the time of the Iron Curtain. I was met at the airport by a concert manager who chatted to me in the taxi en-route to my hotel. Essentially, the cosy chat turned out to be an interrogation as she delved into my history and managed to mention the fact that I knew a defector from the East! Amazing what spies can find out these days. She dropped me at the best hotel in the CSSR and I ran in, caught the lift and dumped my gear down. The room seemed odd; I had never seen so many mirrors, two walls full of them. The heat was intense and I decided to go downstairs for coffee and returned via the lift. At Reception, I realized that I had left my Czech money in my room and had no choice but to go back there. As I stepped out of the lift and approached my door, I heard the lock turn! Stepping back into a doorway, I waited with baited breath as a tall man in a dark suit slowly peered out of my door wearing dark glasses! He scanned the corridor, came out, locked my door and fortunately, strode off in the other direction: Secret Police already on my tail!

I checked my gear and noticed that my sunglasses had been moved but nothing had been taken. Downstairs at Reception, I asked for directions to the Lounge and a large man nearby suddenly got up from his chair, folded his paper and walked ahead of me. He was my spy, my own James Bond and eventually, I noticed him in shops, bars, cafes: you name it, if I was there, he was there! Next night, I gave a concert and, true to form he was there, this time applauding vigorously! He did not call backstage after the encores but a rather attractive, middle-aged lady did step back to shake my hand; her English was impeccable....

"Mr Smith, it was a wonderful concert. We are all so pleased to see you here. Please let me introduce my daughter...."

A stunningly beautiful young woman stepped forward. The mother spoke....
> *"My daughter speaks excellent English and German. She is a musician and would like to study in England....she is not married!"*

The young beauty smiled at me and I waited for the inevitable question....
> *"Are YOU married Mr Smith?"*

Welcome to Prague, get James Bond after you and then get married, I thought!

Everyone piled out of the concert hall and headed for my hotel where a small reception had been arranged; and a surprise for me too. The large man was inside already waiting, cameras flashed and huge bunches of flowers were hoisted upon me and eventually we all sat down chatting and drinking. I talked with Ray Guerra from Cuba who had also had a 'room visit' and, on looking at the bar, I noticed the large man: he was actually smiling at me! As he smiled, he pointed to his left and there stood a fantastically beautiful Slavonic woman in a split-skirt smiling....at me! She turned to one side, still smiling and pushed her leg forwards revealing the entire leg. Now it all clicked: my room, the mirrors....on the ceiling too! I was being set up....Blackmail is a major part of espionage and I was staring the problem in the face. I smiled at the thought of it all and the Eastern beauty swung around to face me, looking better than any 'Bond-Girl' and she pointed at me, curling her finger. I had been warned to expect such as this and so I carried on drinking and talking to my friends until the large man seemed to mutter an angry oath and turned to the girl and dismissed her with a wave of his hand.

Going behind the Curtain once more, Hungary was my next stop as I boarded the British Airways flight to Budapest, another wonderful city in Eastern Europe. I was there to play several events and one of these I will never forget. During the third week of my stay, an organiser asked me to be ready next day by 3pm for a journey into the mountains. On the dot of three, a Volkswagen drew up I jumped in and off we went. By 6pm we could see mountains ahead and though the driver spoke minimal English, we had actually spoken en-route. I asked him about the venue....
> *"You will play in a castle....it was Attila the Hun's castle. He killed all of the Romans here! Do you know of him?"*

Of course, Attila's name is synonymous with death and destruction but I did get a potted history from this driver and it turns out that Attila got bad press in reality. A harsh warrior who could be cruel, but also quite wise and just, when the occasion demanded it. We sped onwards towards the castle of the King of The Huns as the blood-red disc of the sun touched the mountains ahead. Gnarled tree-roots criss-crossed our path making driving uncomfortable and an eerie mist seeped from the forests on each side, giving a distinct 'Dracula' feel to the journey. We halted at a crossroads and a peasant woman in black shawl, carrying twigs turned as the car horn hooted a warning; to say that she was wizened would be a compliment.

Other shapes appeared by the road shuffling along in the mist giving an almost Medieval quality to the scene and above all, the huge sun hung in the sky, still baking down on all....I felt as though I had moved into a time-warp! My driver burst into life....

"ATTILA!!! THE CASTLE....NO PROBLEM!"

as he pointed up ahead to the flickering lights on the mountainside. We both laughed at his sudden outburst but our laughter evaporated when up ahead, out of the forest stepped an armed man brandishing a machine gun! Jamming on the brakes, the driver let out an expletive and I thought that we were going to be ransomed: not long before, such an event had occurred in the East. As we slowed down, the man turned and signalled us to switch off and I saw the red star on his tunic...."Russians" said the driver. My watch showed 7pm and I pointed to the time; the driver simply shrugged and looked ahead at the misty mountains. Time went by and I studied my watch knowing that the concert was due to start at 8pm. To our right beyond some trees, I could hear noises rather like tractor engines and all at once, the sound made an awesome crescendo. The noise became deafening and we could see and hear large machines smashing through the forest. In an instant, the shapes emerged into the open....Russian tanks by the dozen, engines screaming an ear-splitting roar, red stars emblazoned on the turrets as they thundered across the clearing leaving only yards to the nearest tank! The front rank of about ten tanks levelled their huge, long barrels at the trees on the left and ten blinding-orange flashes joined an almighty clap of thunder as the trees disintegrated....LIVE AMMO indeed! Simultaneously, the second rank closed up and turned their guns up across our heads and the roar left me deaf and took my speech away as the car bodily lifted up its front wheels with the shock-wave! The earth was shaking, the noise even greater than imaginable as more tanks crashed forwards and clumps of earth and small pebbles rained down on our protection, the Volkswagen. The tank-tracks hit the road, tearing lumps from the surface and the dust and fumes clouded the view of bedlam. Not the ideal prelude to a quiet guitar recital! They all dashed on destroying a fence and splitting trees, branches, soil, twigs hurtling into the air again. As the tanks entered the woods, the noise dropped a little and a sickly smell of engine fumes hung around the devastated clearing. We were both stunned. Never have I witnessed such a display of brute force: imagine for a moment being in one of those colossal tank-battles in Russia during the War as over 1,000 of these monsters charged about the place! It must have been the nightmare of the century; Hell on Wheels.

After this deluge of noise, a single Personnel Carrier moved out from the right towards the road and an officer jumped out and began inspecting the roadway. A soldier with a bucket joined him and so together, they filled in the holes gouged by the tanks....then drove off into the woods. The soldier, who was by now safely standing near to our car, waved us forwards and we bumped over the fresh tarmac and onwards, hurrying to the castle with the time approaching 7.30pm: shocked, confused and deaf! The castle itself was a ruin, only the central hall was intact and, as I quickly entered the doorway, the Curator stepped forward to greet me. His news was good; the concert was delayed until 9pm. The delay gave me time to survey the hall. It was a large, box-shaped room lined with heavy slabs of the finest dark wood and on one side, a vicious-looking sword over five feet long hung down the wall. Across from the sword, a real Roman helmet in burnished gold glittered in the rays of the setting sun and a Roman dagger hung beneath. The castle was not exactly palatial like Hampton Court or The Kremlin but it was obviously a serious and formidable fortress and somehow, the whole ruin, savaged by over one thousand years of battle oozed power, intrigue and menace. Reluctantly, I left the hall to prepare and to attempt to recover my hearing. At nine prompt, The Curator ushered me into the hall: to my astonishment, it was filled to bursting with Russian soldiers! Their black, knee-high boots gleamed and their spurs jangled and the floor shuddered as they snapped to attention on command. The green tunics and gold-braid looked splendid as their swords glinted and the red stars shone like piercing eyes out of the crowd. One each side, the relics of the Romans and Huns reflected the flashes as cameras clicked away. After the concert, a soldier called around to see me. He was the only English-speaking soldier in his unit, a unit that had been in action in Afghanistan. No wonder so many present wore medals. A thought suddenly occurred to me and I told him about the tanks....he interrupted me.

"Yes, I know! We stopped you in our tanks because we had to get back to change our uniforms!"

We both roared with laughter at the idea....a 20-gun salute for the British guest! Before leaving, I returned to the hall to collect my footstool. In the afterglow, the helmet and swords cast eerie shadows along each wall and there seemed to be a distinct 'aura' about the place: the Curator gave me a knowing nod when I mentioned this. If ever there was a Hall of The Mountain King, this was it!

As we departed, I stared back for many minutes until the rugged ruin had disappeared and we were once more on our mock-battlefield. A few kilometres on, the yawning driver slammed on his brakes as another old woman wandered into our path in the mist. She turned, scowling, and in the headlights, her face seemed like a study in witchcraft. The deeply etched lines and furrows stood out like cuts in her flesh as she angrily waved us onwards. Gradually, the mist faded and I sat silent with my impressions as the driver hummed away at a little tune. The rutted tracks bumped and jolted us onwards into the night, towards Budapest and civilisation.

PLAY IT AGAIN, SAM….

Recording, TV, radio, disc, video….these words would have meant nothing to Bach, Mozart, Beethoven, Paganini and Liszt. Their reputation stands firm today, in the main secure through their wonderful compositions and only in a small part due to their legendary powers of performance. By the time Edison propelled music into the Age of Technology, most of the household names in music were dead and gone. We cannot return to hear their actual manner of performance nor indeed can we imitate their mannerisms. Apparently, both Beethoven (keyboards) and Paganini (violin and guitar) broke strings during an evening: Paganini often doing this on purpose to show his skill. Both Bach and Mozart had incredible reading and improvisatory powers and could astonish the musically-literate with reams of notes and pieces off the top of their heads. How was it done, how did it sound? We will never know.

Recording is a relatively modern phenomenon going back some 100 years and, if one listens to the old recordings of Caruso, Granados or Rakhmaninov, it is obvious that it is not always easy to reproduce the very highest playing level during a recording session. Readers who possess a phone-answering machine will know of the frustration of trying to obtain an articulate message from one's own voice….recording is TEN times more difficult. In this chapter, we will go into the recording and television studios, spanning a career of thirty years. Play it again, Sam, _if_ you can!

I was the first guitarist to broadcast for BBC Radio Manchester and, in the early days, the studio was a rabbit warren of offices opposite the Piccadilly Hotel downtown. I walked the bustling corridors meeting Stuart Hall (radio/TV presenter) and a host of other names in the canteen. The producer called me in and there was the studio: thick carpet, acoustic tiles, no real sonority at all. To make matters worse, there were no real editing options, only links in the tape could be made: I would have to play direct, without any errors. The session was a minor success and I returned there on numerous occasions. In 1975, Radio Merseyside asked for a full hour and we selected a local library as a venue for this. Early that evening, I sat with the producer as we dismally listened to the clicking of high-heels over the microphones….the building was still in use. Not to be beaten, we packed and rushed over to Tarleton Village (Lancashire) to the producer's home and had set up once more by 9.30pm. I gritted my teeth and cleared the decks by midnight, arriving home about 1.30am, tired and with a headache.

Up until that date, I had not been on television and I wrote to the BBC and ITV telling them of my scholarship to study at Toronto University on a course with Alirio Diaz and Leo Brouwer, two of the greats in the small world of guitar. I flew off to Canada without receiving replies and once there, I began to work hard, trying to avoid the distractions such as Niagra

MASTERCLASS, TORONTO UNIVERSITY, 1975
Before the CBC microphones, my class with the great Alirio Diaz comes to a close. A long, long way to Canada for lessons but, that's life.

Falls, etc. All too soon, my day came and, in the morning break, a camera-crew hoisted me off to a corner to make an interview and, at the end, the team-leader told me....

"Well thank you Neil. We will be back this afternoon to take your class on tape for national CBC transmission, ok?"

Yes, ok, thanks very much....would you also like to saw off my head? The hot, sticky class went very well, ending with a 'Bravo!' from Maestro Diaz and he invited me for tea later along with his wife. Looking back, it could have been a complete disaster zone. Returning to the UK, I found my (red-haired) wife in a foul mood: the television people had replied in my absence and it was all vague and even negative. In this ranting mood, she phoned the radio/TV people and gave them a piece of her mind! Thankfully, they were in sympathy and she turned to me to say that I was actually going to be on television: soon!

I bought new clothes, practised like mad and soon the day arrived as I sat downtown in the studio, a dark, cool room with the silent cameras clustered around, all pointing inwards at me. I heard footsteps and, turning around I saw a very beautiful woman standing behind me holding a clipboard....

"Hello Neil, my name is Anna Ford and I will introduce you tonight."

The session got started with Anna to one side at a desk reading copy, and she hesitated: my name was wrong! Minutes ticked by as the tapes were rewound: at Union speeds (minimum of 20 minutes to reset) and I sat alone in the gloom as the lights were dimmed. Then we were ready again and... once more, my name was not correct! The tension mounted and I felt like a deer about to be shot; and actually knowing it. Third time lucky and I started off, sweating hands (not normal for me) and strange sounds all around me as the camera cables swished around the floor. I neared the end of my piece and suddenly, in my ear I heard....

"Camera Two: side shot....five seconds!"

This totally threw me, a noise from the headset of a cameraman ruined the whole thing and I ground to a halt, completely distracted. A voice from the Gods boomed out....

*"What the ******* **** are you doing? We need this today, not tomorrow!"*

The producer emerged on set and spoke to Anna and myself; she had to leave to read the news and so, her part was ended and we shook hands and apologized....to each other! The next take got it in one and, as the lights faded, some mild applause filtered from the rear; there stood several 'characters' from Coronation Street including Gail, Rita, Eddie and old Percy Sugden. They were having a break on-set and Percy leapt over to say how much he enjoyed Spanish Guitar music. I ran back to the make-up room to clean up and met Betty and Hilda from The Street and they too wanted to

69

watch my playing on TV that night. I dashed off through the rush hour and just made it home to see the broadcast: Television at last!

More TV and radio followed, some of it abroad, but here in the UK, I knew that I had to crack the BBC Audition Procedure in order to play on national radio. The BBC form was formidable: applicants had to send off at least two main programmes, plus press cuttings (unedited) plus any diplomas etc, plus any supporting letters. This would lead to a Test Recording which was later broadcast to a panel who voted in secret on the quality of each artist. Thumbs up, thumbs down AND failure meant that a black mark would go against your name for the future: radio and TV concerts could not be offered to such a player, maybe ever. I did complete a test and, to my delight, Michael Berkeley selected a large chunk of my programme for one of his Pick of The Week slots. I was on the way up!

1982, and The Guernsey Festival held a BBC-promoted week of events with stars like Val Doonican, Moira Anderson and the BBC Phil along with me playing the opening concert. The concert was what was known as a 'Deferred-Relay' whereby an event is recorded unedited and is played back later for broadcast. As part of the deal, I had to appear on the afternoon chat-slot on Radio Guernsey and, since it was only an interview, I did not take my guitar (bad move). We sat around a large desk, the radio presenter, the concert producer, me and another man whose purpose became clear later on. The chat centered on my work and life and then turned to the subject of 'old' music. I mentioned a little about old instruments, the problems of playing them, the poor state of repairs….the presenter took his opportunity.

"I'm glad that you mentioned that, Neil, because here in studio we have a guest who just happens to have such a guitar…."

The silent 'guest' came to life, producing out of a bin-bag an old, cracked guitar with rusting strings. It was described in detail on air, a point, which I'm sure, was totally lost on the listeners. Without warning, the presenter's jolly voice pipped in….

"How about playing it, Neil? Perhaps a piece from the programme tonight?"

Gareth Walters, the concert producer was mortified and he signalled a wave across his throat! I too sat there horrified as the owner of this antique gently passed the guitar across the green-baize table, live on radio! I moved off into a corner as the bumbling presenter fumbled his way along and fury showed in Gareth's face. The creaking tuning-pegs were 150 years old, the strings seemed older as I struggled, trying hard to make less noise and fuss: things were bad enough! After what seemed like an age, the guitar was tolerably tuned and I did play a little piece on air; if you possess a recording, please hide it away somewhere in the dark!

I travelled often to Scotland in those days and to the Lakes staying often with great friends in Ulverston and Carlisle. Border Television is based in that city and late one night, I recorded some short pieces for interlude music: Marisa Robles, the harpist had just finished an identical set and so the studio left the chairs, lighting etc just as before, the session thus concluded very quickly indeed. I was invited to the Executive Suite and there met Derek Batey (of TV fame in Mr & Mrs) who was in charge of events up at Border and he asked me to join him for a giant season of bookings all around Britain. Sadly, my own travels could not accommodate the tour....I was due to play in five countries over the next seven weeks myself. After a hearty meal at the hotel, I set off on a horrible, misty night down the M6 on a journey, which seemed endless. I noticed car lights behind me, following at exactly my speed, maybe even trailing me for some unknown reason. All at once, the siren sounded, blue lights flashed and the Motorway Police pulled me over. Standing in the rain and fog, the officer checked my details and shone his torch into the back of my car. Seeing the guitars, he asked if I was 'THE' Neil Smith who had played on BBC Radio 3 the week previously. I confirmed his question and he immediately said....

"Great....can I have your autograph for your son? He is guitar-mad and he really likes hearing you play!"

I signed the wet piece of paper and smiled as I looked ahead towards the dark, folding hills around Tebay. How bizarre I thought, giving policemen an autograph at two in the morning in such a venue!

Today, many celebs turn up for chat shows with their latest video or disc and are quite happy to talk away the hours without having to actually get out there and 'Perform' with a capital P. And, being honest, how many of them can actually do it up front, on 'Live TV' in front of millions? Very few indeed and yet, classical players are expected to take this stance without turning a hair: a boiling hot studio, hundreds in the studio audience and ten million watching at home. Fancy risking YOUR career on a chance like this? On one spin of a wheel; no retakes? Without preparation, most people would actually collapse under the tension. One problem today is that pre-concert publicity is essential all round and a 'chat' on radio is worth a whole lot of revenue.

In Los Angeles, the radio presenter John Schnieder asked me to appear live on his show on the morning of a concert. We chatted away for over a half-hour and John warned me to be ready to play an item lasting 7 minutes. I placed the headphones on and got started and all went fine for maybe five minutes. I could see John thru the studio glass nodding away as I played on and on. With no warning, the headphones started to slip forwards off my head! Both hands engaged, I could do nothing as I sat there, frozen to the microphone. John rose out of his seat, intending to burst in and correct the upcoming catastrophe but, it was too late. The phones fell across the strings and my right hand as I just for a split second lost a note and went on to finish the piece. John gave a thumbs-up through the glass and simply told the listeners....

"Well that was Neil playing live and you would NEVER believe what has just happened here in studio!"

In 1983, I was booked to play on live television in a special show called Friday Night Live. Edward Fox the actor was on and Pattie Boulaye the singer too, the whole show hung together due to the signature tune. This was always 'arranged' for the guest instrumentalist who was instructed to play at various cue-points along the way. As the critical Friday loomed ahead, I had a call from the producer of the show to see how the 'music' was shaping up: my news was bad. Basically, the music had not arrived! Wednesday evening, a call came through from a hospital, the composer was ill and had agreed to dictate (by phone) the whole set of pieces over to me! A crazy plan but it worked and after three HOURS of writing, I had the outline of the show including timings (critical for live TV). The Friday night came and I was well aware of the tension as I walked into the producer's office. <u>Everyone</u> including the tea-lady was so kind and wanted to help me to keep things placid; the music was the 'hinge' of the whole show, the timings even more critical than I had first thought since we had to accommodate advert-timings too. We ran the show in rehearsal and it went very well and, contrary to the usual run of things, the live show went even better than expected and great sighs of relief surged around the bar afterwards.

Playing live and joining in with other musicians can be a deadly game, especially if the music is tough. Booked to play once more with that great orchestra, the C.B.S.O. I made my way down the night before to Birmingham for an 11am direct-broadcast of the famous Rodrigo Concerto from the Town Hall. Atarah Ben-Tovim, my great friend introduced the event to the packed house, my wife and both children sat up in the Gods. Guy Woolfenden conducted that day and as I came onto the stage, Guy nodded to me to allow me time to settle. After a few moments, he raised his baton and....out of nowhere came a little voice....

"That's my Daddy!"

The whole crowd roared with laughter as my youngest child shrank in horror as all eyes turned to her on the balcony. Guy simply smiled and we went on, equal applause for father and daughter that day.

Once more in Birmingham, I was scheduled to play a solo event one evening and radio called me in for a 5-minute-special, just before the news at 6pm. I sat warming my fingers in the cold and, at 5.52pm the producer called in to see me. His words....

"This piece you are playing; is it copyright? If it is then we don't want it, you'll just have to play something older!"

Just imagine this setting, three minutes to go and trapped with no extra music, no extra time to rehearse and then this....my helper Brian Penny could only sit there and say WOW! I had a few 'regulars' up my sleeve and fortunately was able to change, almost with a smile....almost!

My ultimate Radio-Horror story came on a BBC Maida Vale session in the Eighties. Booked for a three-hour stint before the microphones, I arrived on a chilly day at 1pm to warm my fingers up for the 2pm start. During little breaks in my practice, I looked in through the studio glass now and again to see Dame Janet Baker singing away, Purcell judging from some of the faint noises I heard through the doors. At 1.50pm, Gareth arrived and, seeing the studio in use, he looked puzzled and went in to speak with the producer in the box. He emerged looking more than puzzled: our session had been moved to Broadcasting House, a taxi-ride away in busy traffic! Off we set and on arrival, we noticed workmen drilling on the edge wall, approximately alongside the Concert Hall. It was 2.45pm and I sat before the microphones and knocked the first two items down without retakes, without edits. Gareth walked down the hall towards me: the third item could not be taken. One week previous, a player had played that item 'live' on Radio 3 as an encore and the policy was such that consecutive re-runs of pieces could not take place. Could I think of another 5-minute piece: right away with no music! I sat for a few minutes deep in thought, wishing that I had stayed home in Manchester. Suddenly, an item came to me and we set off and part way through, Gareth interrupted me over the intercom; a 'ticking' noise could be heard in the console. Everything halted and we walked around the studio-hall several times until it became clear what was wrong. The overhead heaters had gone off for some reason and in the cooling process, the elements were obviously making the noise. The only thing to do was wait....and wait as the 5pm deadline approached.

Long after 3.30, the 'ticking' ended and we set out once more on our journey. Into the final items, Gareth called out once more; this time a 'whistling-noise' could be heard and, in the silence, I heard it loud and clear. Again, we tramped around the hall, looking under seats, ears to the walls, everywhere in fact but without success. On the point of giving up, I walked past the exit-door and noticed the sound increase in volume. Outside, sat happily chewing away on a sandwich was an electrician reading The Sun newspaper, his kettle busily boiling away on a little stove! Above his head, a bright neon-sign flashed....
RECORDING IN PROGRESS....SILENCE PLEASE!
After giving the guy a verbal roasting, we went back in to wind the session up and at 4.55pm, I finished much to the admiration of the BBC Choir who had crammed their way into the recording booth. I just made the train in time and bought more than a few Carlsberg Specials, the great standby for those moments in one's day....those special moments of peace and harmony.

TALES OF
THE UNEXPECTED....

Maybe I could have titled most of the chapters in this book Tales of The Unexpected; maybe even the whole book! Certainly I never anticipated the events so far described but some happenings do not fit into the current mode of the book and so, they exist as odds and ends, small stories of things and people and places, not connected by theme but linked through a common denominator....Me!

The reader will by now know that I play or have played almost all musical styles in current vogue and, at one time, I studied Flamenco music. This is not 'classical' in the traditional sense and yet, there can be certain fused-areas where the two styles coexist happily. Rafael de Sevilla was a fine dancer and a superb entertainer. He often took on stage a small poodle which could dance to the snappy rhythms of the guitars and castanets; I hasten to add that the dog was extremely well cared for, often eating at the best restaurants after a show!

One night, Rafael phoned me from London; he wanted me to join him in a show at the Nottingham Playhouse, a Flamenco Spectacular. The only problem was that I had to confirm immediately since posters and programmes were to be printed next day. For over twenty minutes, I tried to spell out my name over the phone but no way could he write it down exactly. On the appointed night, I drove to Nottingham and, on entering the theatre, I looked at the huge poster. Nowhere was my name to be seen but, a guitarist called 'Niolo Larrrcon' was playing my pieces instead! I went around the back and found Rafael; he was sorry, that was the best name and nearest name to mine he could find! No matter, we went on with the show and in the interval, we went out back onto a verandah, drinking and laughing about the name-change. Soon, the small theatre made a break and over towards us came a man in the garb of a priest; smoking a cigar and drinking a pint of beer! The priest expressed his concern about the 'hot' night in the most colourful language one could imagine and Rafael, dumbstruck for a moment, eyed him up and down with contempt....

"Mother in Heaven sir: you are an insult to your cloth. And you are drinking the beer, smoking the cigar and saying these foul words. The Holy Father would cast you out from our Church!"

As Rafael spoke these very words, the newcomer began to pull off his false beard and collar: he was an actor! We almost tumbled off the balcony laughing as Rafael rolled his eyes at his mistake!

Going up north in winter, I was due to play at a castle for a musical evening and the snow and ice increased as I moved onward into the darkness. The castle appeared as a twinkling set of lights far ahead and I drove into the courtyard to be met by a servant who grabbed my bags and ushered me upstairs quickly. On reaching the room, he put my bags down outside, pushed the door open but did not go into the room. This seemed odd to me but, I went in and began to check the guitar, music, clothes, etc. A knock came later at the door; a maid with a 5-course meal ready prepared and she too pushed the trolley up to the door but did not step inside. She did ask in a halting voice....

"Is everything all right then?"

I confirmed that it was and she seemed happy to go. The room had a rather luxurious appearance and the food was high-class but there was something strange about the place. Even so, I went down and played the first part of my evening and later, in the interval, I met the owner/manager of the estate. He asked me the same thing....

"Everything all right up there then?"

I said that it was all ok and he asked if I had 'seen' anybody up there: I hesitated and asked what he meant....

"Well, we have all seen a lady in that room a rather old, ghostly figure and we just wondered if you had noticed the same person!"

Needless to say, I kept my eyes peeled on my return; I saw nothing but there was certainly an odd feeling about the place. No doubt, I will return there and can tell the reader about my next 'experience' in another book.

Playing a concert at a church in the wilds of Westmorland, my driver Denis and I arrived early to liase with a lighting-engineer. When he arrived, we found out that the church had no power supply, no water, no toilets, no vestry, no changing rooms....nothing at all! I had set off in a less than ready state thinking to smarten up at the venue! We spoke with the vicar (who lived miles away) and he suggested that we use the Phone Box opposite the church yard for changing, shaving and anything else! Sure enough, there was a red phone-box across the way and I allowed the other guy to go in first. He changed and, as he came out, people started to arrive early for the recital. I went into the box and struggled to change my shirt, foolishly putting on my starch-white concert shirt and <u>then</u> shaving with a dry-razor! The little, blurred mirror was in part glazed over and I cut myself to ribbons leaving blood on my collar with nothing to clean it up. True to form, as soon as I decided to change into my concert suit, a woman (not a man) walked up to the box demanding to use the phone to tell her husband the time of the concert finish! I shuffled out of the box, half-dressed and stood in the evening air, no rehearsal for me at all. When the recital had ended, I went home in my tuxedo, preferring this to another episode in the 'changing-room'.

Thinking of the North reminds me of the time I caught the last express to Glasgow on a New Year's Eve. Heading for Preston, my nearest city, I wanted to rest up all through the journey: no such luck. As the train jerked forwards from Euston, a dishevelled man literally banged into the glass window, startling the poor elderly lady sat opposite me....he vanished out of sight, possibly under the wheels! The old lady asked....

"Do you think he is all right?"

I opened the upper window and looked out; he had gone <u>but</u>, I did hear the door bang shut way back. A few minutes later, he arrived at our compartment door, looking for all the world like the actor Alan Bates in Whistle Down The Wind (a tramp). He fell into a corner and snored away for ages until, as the train pulled in to Rugby, he suddenly woke up. He asked me our whereabouts and I told him and, on hearing this, he started to rummage in his large coat pockets: out came six bottles of Johnnie Walker Black Label whisky! He waved a bottle at me....

"Dinna ya want some o' this?"

he shouted, the old lady cowered in the other corner. He offered her a 'wee-dram' direct from the bottle but,no, she did not rise to the bait. Settling down, he swigged away at a bottle and then started to tell me of his life in the 'oil industry' in the Middle East: he wanted to make it home to 'Bonnie Scotland' for midnight and I understood his need for this. Soon, we talked of our adventures and he thought that I was actually more crazy than he was; I took a bottle from him and started my steady decline into ruin. The old lady looked extremely restless and only held on to her seat because it was 'Reserved'....she would have been far better in another compartment. I wandered off to the Dining Car which was about to close (WHY does this always happen?) and I asked for some plastic cups and took them away with me. In my absence, the lady had started talking to our new-found friend and when I entered in with the cups she willingly joined in, her destination being Penrith. Soon, she was happily drinking away and laughing at us both and I poured out the liquor into her beaker as she slurred her words more and more with every mile that passed. The Scotsman saw my guitar: he wanted me to play Auld Lang Syne there on the train and so, I made him change seats (NEVER play facing the direction of travel!) and we set off, the old lady singing away, more pleased than before. As this carousing continued, I forgot that my car was waiting at the station....I would have to get a cab home or a bus or a train! Eventually, the man sank into a stupor, the old lady was giggling away and I stepped off the train just in time to catch a local train home. They were both asleep as they left Preston Station; I hope that they made it!

In Turkey, I made the most of my stay, seeing the sights, getting cheap shirts, and even watching a 'belly-dancer'....who actually came from Essex! I love wandering off into strange places, the sights and sounds always fascinate me even though (as we have seen) this can lead to problems. I went off to a local market where produce was sold and various items used by the town population. Wandering around for hours, the fruit and the vegetables were so unusual for me; never had I seen some of the varieties on display, the sun baked down on me as I walked and walked the lines of lovely items for sale. Soon I saw a stall with what seemed to be musical instruments and, true enough, there it was, a shop in the midst of everything else, totally unrelated to the surroundings, a few clarinets, a mandolin and many Turkish instruments hanging up on the breeze. I pointed to one particular instrument and the man called over to his pal on the other stall, asking him to translate. The smallest item there was called a 'Dura' with six-strings close together rather like a mandolin and the man quickly tuned it and pushed me to one side as if to say....

"Forget it man, you know nothing of such things!"

I listened as he tuned and figured out that it was like part (only part) of a guitar. He scrabbled around on some rudimentary tune; to be honest, it was rubbish and I looked back at him and took The Dura from his grip. Taking his plectra (rather like a small plectrum) I hammered into a solo item and his eyes shot forwards....his friends gathered around, clapping and cheering exactly in time. Pretty soon, the whole avenue was clapping and laughing and jumping around as I strummed on under the hot sun. And I played some of the Turkish tunes that the "Essex' girl had danced to the night before. I guess that really, on that day, I could have asked for the Moon in that bazaar but, all I needed was The Dura. The man held up a note which I knew to be valued at £20 Sterling. I laughed and he made a 'division' sign saying that he would cut it in half: ok then, £10 for a Dura....I accepted and the Dura is here with me in my home today.

I travelled often to Europe with the recorder virtuoso John Turner and on one occasion, we went to Wolfenbüttel, a wonderful town near to Hamlyn....Pied Piper territory! We landed at Hannover the same day and made our way over to the town, settled into the hotel and went out for a look around. The place was astonishing; really, it can be said that nothing in the UK can equal this place with its narrow streets, wooden houses (which almost fall onto each other) signed-shops, and real, 'Medieval' atmosphere. We wandered far and wide around town even though our concert was within a few hours. Then we were taken to the palace of the Duke of Brunswick, a great and mighty Prince in the time of the Renaissance. His chief musician had been Michael Praetorius (1571-1621) a remarkable man whose music is still in vogue today (fancy a bet with me if The Beatles will still be in vogue in 400 years?). We played the recital and the Bürgermeister called in to see us afterwards. He knew about Praetorius of course since the composer had been Kapellmeister to the Duke in 1612 and had produced a fantastic collection of dances. A pass was available next day if we wanted to use it and so we went down into the vaults (dungeons) of the Schloss Wolfenbüttel to see the treasures there. The Praetorius items were on regular display but I wanted to see something else. The Director of the Museum showed me the computer roll and on it, I saw the name of John Dowland, the greatest Lute player of his day (possibly of all time). The Director ordered his music to be brought to me and I was sent to a small, glass room, watched by a security guard as I waited for the manuscript from 1603 AD. A lady soon came along with a trolley with the priceless Dowland copies placed on top. The guard checked the checklist and allowed her in: gloves to hold the actual book and pass it over to me. I placed the great book on the desk in front of me and the cover said it all....

THESAURUS HARMONICUS. 1603

This was one of the 'Bibles' of music literature in the Renaissance and on that very day in 1987, I held it in my hands. I decided to open the front cover as the Security Guard watched me closely and the pages actually creaked and groaned as I pushed the leaves apart. Using my tracing-list, I soon found the Dowland item I wanted to see and stared for many minutes at the manuscript....one of only THREE copies in the entire world.

John and I later returned to Germany to play a special recital for German and British ministers. We arrived early and started to rehearse knowing that ministers from Bonn and London were en-route that day. We began to rehearse in the hall and suddenly, a door opened and in came a man, dressed in plain clothes, he began to scan the room: up, down, side, back, under, above, front, back,....whatever way you selected, he had that covered. The whole operation went on for many minutes and soon John had to ask his purpose: he was the top-security Chief of Police and his job was to search today for explosives! We did play the recital as scheduled but I was rather glad to return to the hotel that particular night.

I played a good deal in Norway for a time and I met a good number of leading Norwegian musicians. Kjell Marcussen had written some guitar works and I wanted to meet him there: on site, in his home. John, Margaret and I voyaged over the North Sea in order to give the premiere of a new work, a Viking Sonata, which I had asked for long before. The inspiration for such a theme was my visit to a Viking stronghold and village where a genuine attempt had been made to reconstruct that amazing past. As we wandered around the Viking Ship Museum in Oslo, I prompted Kjell to examine this Viking past and to try to discover a piece of Viking music of great intensity. Kjell worked hard to find a real Viking theme but alas, such things do not exist; let me say now that Vikings did play various instruments but, none of the actual music seems to have survived. He produced a great work, a large work and we played it in the Viking Museum for a video sat beneath those awesome ships; blackened hulls standing over us as we played; 80 fierce men to a ship, swords, shields, daggers and the like all ready to hit out at the already-terrified enemy (sometimes US!). The reality of these ships hit me as we stood before them to record the music, skeleton-like shafts of black-wood standing bare against the sky and set in a museum as we played out our latest 'piece' under the very structure and bones of the ship. And afterwards, I walked around to see the swords, the daggers, the gold, silver and jewellery on display there, staggering to see so late in our century....we think we know it all and yet, such craftsmanship has to be seen to be believed.

THE OSEBERG VIKING SHIP, OSLO.
This amazing ship is 22 metres long and is surrounded by swords, axes and relics.
Copyright: University Museum of Cultural Heritage - University of Oslo, Norway.
Photographer: Eirik Irgens Johnsen.

Go West, Young Man….that was stated at the start of this volume and it can be a trigger for all kinds of activity in today's world. In the late Eighties, I flew across the USA from New York to Los Angeles and the journey was remarkable to say the least. My flight took off shortly after midday heading out across Virginia, Kentucky (green, green, green) and on into Arkansas (what roads….miles and miles in a straight line!) and onwards into the West. On such flights, the sun 'travels with you' and the actual daylight seems to change very little as the aircraft speeds onwards. Even though that was my first time across the USA, I felt tired and nodded off after my fillet-steak and champagne. The captain came on the intercom….

"Ladies and gentlemen I'm afraid that I have some bad news. We have been diverted today and will arrive in Los Angeles behind schedule. The compensation is that we will take a route along the Grand Canyon which I'm sure will more than make up for your delay."

I blinked my eyes and looked around but little seemed to be happening until a huge, red cliff steered into view on the right side. Even at our height, the Canyon was colossal and we drifted slowly along that great divide, the Colorado seeming so 'red' as it flowed like a vein through the massive walls of the great cleft. Our pilot seemed to have a sense of the dramatic and he often tipped the jet to the right or left so that we could see this marvel edge-on as it were. The views were often quite amazing and an air-stewardess sat down next to me to look over my shoulder.

"WOW!!!....I've never, ever seen this before," (she said). "I feel lost in all of this desert....really, you are seeing something very unusual here!"

And she moved over to the other side of the aircraft as a new vista came into view, the red chasms turning blue, green, purple, and almost any colour as the jet dipped in and out of the canyon radius. So many thoughts crossed my mind then, home, kids, the music, my journey, and, first and foremost my (late) wife who could not be with me. And still the incredible scenery went on and on, making even the stewardesses gasp out at the vast and awesome power of Nature stretching below us. Again, the red, monster-cliffs rose below our jet and, even though we were many miles high, this seemed as nothing to the canyon as it reached up towards us. The Colorado snaking in and out of the crags, foaming here and there even at this height as to the West, the sun baked down on us all mercilessly. I'm not sure whether the Grand Canyon is actually one of the 'Wonders of The World' but I can say that, on that day, everyone in the aircraft felt that the Canyon had astonished us all; the silence during the trip was most unusual as people had gazed open-jawed at the whole spectacle. The pilot was right….it had more than made up for our delay.

Travelling to Germany, I had an invite to play at the castle which hosted the superb festival held by guitarist Siegfried Behrend in Bavaria. In absolutely magnificent surroundings with Teutonic armour and flags, guitarists could come along for an eight-week festival of guitar. My concert was to be in a church outside the walls but I stayed over in the castle for a few days. On the first morning, a terrible screaming noise awoke me, truly frightening to a sleeping person; I looked around from my window but saw nothing unusual. Speaking with Siegfried about this noise, he asked me to follow him into the courtyard near the gate and there, chained to the walls were six giant Condors! These massive birds were his 'pets' and also his guards since they could reach out with their enormous wings and hit out with great force at anyone who dared to go past them! Each day, a man brought a barrow full of sheep-heads and other 'delicacies' for the huge, hungry creatures and they let out wild shrieks as they devoured their meal. These bone-crunching birds could break limbs with one sweep of a wing and not even the bravest reader would have gone within striking distance, believe me!

Opera horror-stories abound but unfortunately, the guitar is rarely involved in such productions and my anecdotes would be less than vivid. I did play in the revival of the great opera Beatrice & Benedict by Hector Berlioz. He had been a guitarist (as had Schubert, Paganini, Rossini and many more) and he often included a part for the guitar in his musical ventures. The part in Beatrice was cleverly written; at one point, Berlioz had a choir, two female singers and a little guitar playing all at once! According to his plan, we set the Welsh National Chorus way back at the exit doors, the duo sang to the side and I played out front to project the small guitar sound. Two conductors directed via a video-link in order to synchronize parts. This worked very well on opening night but I was worried about another piece later on: the part had the word Guitares written on the cover but the 's' was crossed out! I had to somehow play it solo and I sat in the interval struggling with what should really have been a shared part. Plugging away at this, I failed to notice someone looking over my shoulder and the familiar voice interrupted me....

"I say....were you playing out there? Very good that and nice to hear a guitar in this setting. The whole work is superb!"

I looked around into the face of Sir Donald Sinden, the great actor. He had come along to this production especially and he told me of his interest in opera and of his travels around and about to see opera 'live' on stage. As the weeks went by, the work eased into a routine and one particular piece always seemed to go well, a song for Baritone, Guitar and THREE trumpets! In the interval, I often went off to the local pub with the brass players and one night, I left them playing darts and wound my way back into the crammed orchestra pit: two orchestras combined for this giant work. The trumpeters did not show and soon, the cues appeared for our 'ensemble' to prepare. The conductor pointed his illuminated baton at me as the dialogue wound onwards and I looked at him and shook my head, pointing to three empty chairs beside me; his eyes almost popped out of his head! It was pointless to try to halt things and he gave the downbeat and I commenced....alone.

Suddenly, feet could be heard scuffling through the pit, pushing and shoving their way through, the lads rushed in and sat down with about five seconds to go to their entry, the conductor's face lighting up with joy as never before!

Some events can cause even the most secure person real trauma, often for no logical reason. On one of my evenings at the Royal Festival Hall, London, I donned my tail-suit and went out to view the stage via the secret spy-hole. The huge building was full to bursting and I adjusted my tie in the mirror as a uniformed attendant looked on....

"Everything ok then? Full-house tonight out there....enough to make anybody nervous. Why, last week I had to help one pianist to tie his own tie! You don't seem worried...."

I couldn't help thinking; had he been picked for this job or was he a volunteer?

Instrumentalists tend to work at a career in a different way to a vocalist....they begin singing in groups, choirs, etc and progress onward until they are considered high enough to be a soloist. With an instrument, the opposite is true as one often begins playing solo and makes progress towards being a Concerto-Soloist, playing very difficult items with symphonic orchestras. The road that climbs to the top through this particular gateway is indeed tricky and of all of the thousands who take up a serious musical career, very few will actually work on stage with the greatest orchestras. Everyone, regardless of talent, has to work with local orchestras first in order to establish a name. Once, I worked with a nice, amateur outfit and at rehearsal, we took a tea break and I walked back past the strings; a bass-player who seemed at least 85 years old leaned over and grabbed my arm....

"Very nice young man, very nice. We have never worked with a guitar before and this Rodrigo is a good piece."

So saying, he let go of my arm and I walked off; but not before I heard him turn to his 'older' bassist....

"You know that bit where e' wants us to drop down a shade? Well, I'm damned if I'm doing that on Sunday! All my family are coming along and by hell, they'll hear me play!"

Reaching the tea-urn, I casually mentioned this to the conductor who was well aware of their attitude and intention....he simply shook his head and muttered...."Reprobates!"

The Sound of Music....a show which features the guitar of von Trapp on film, disc, stage, and yet, how many of the actors actually play anything? Some years ago, an actor gave me a call: could I teach him the guitar in six weeks? Of course, the answer was negative, a response which cheered him somewhat and he proceeded to outline an idea, namely that I would play and he would mime. The intended lesson costs would go as my fee for the two-week run. We met and I started to show him the style, the grip, the general outline of playing and he posed in a mirror to check for maximum effect. We rehearsed via the conductor who signalled between us so precisely that it was often difficult to tell that the guy was miming. On Opening Night, it all went well and I walked out into the foyer during the interval for a breath of air. Captain von Trapp was there, walking around, friends slapping his back and one rather stunning lady congratulated him on his 'wonderful' guitar playing: he responded….

"*Nothing my dear, I just picked it up in a few weeks you know. No trouble at all!*"

So saying, he turned around only to see me standing nearby: this was the one and only time I ever saw an actor blush!

One bleak winter, I stayed over in a British Army hostel in Berlin where the security-tight guards held all visitors at machine-gun point, scrutinized documents and frisked everyone before <u>considering</u> admittance! My next concert was beyond the Iron Curtain and they stared long and hard at my multi-visa passport before calling HQ and allowing me inside. Next day, I jumped into a taxi which finally dropped me off at a strange airport, not the regular international building. The leaden-grey sky to the East looked menacing, the icy, wind-swept tarmac seemed positively dangerous for travel and I boarded the jet and sat in the cold cabin; delayed again, doors fully open, no warmth or comfort. Soon, I heard a commotion at the front of the jet; German Security Police came on board with vicious-looking dogs, snarling around under the seats and up and down the aisles. The officers all held hand-detectors and they asked severe questions, searched every nook and cranny, each bag, box, case, coat….everything. An air- hostess told me calmly….

"*We have had a bomb alert – better safe than sorry!*"

I couldn't have agreed more and felt a horrible sense of claustrophobia creeping over me….why not evacuate the aircraft?

We stayed on board and eventually clearance was given. The jet soared off over East Berlin along the special air-corridor which had been negotiated with the Eastern Bloc. This zone was policed by armed East German fighters and any pilot-error meant truly grave problems for us all, perhaps even death. Our delay sent the aircraft on a wild detour and we passed on into unfamiliar territory as the snow-covered fields gave way to the occasional farm or village. As the jet turned east, I noticed a small hamlet below and something made me ask the hostess about the aircraft position. She returned saying that the captain had said that we had just passed over Cöthen. The town is not famous except for the fact that the great composer Johann Sebastian Bach lived there and had written some of his greatest music during his service with the Prince of Anhalt-Cöthen. As sunlight suddenly flashed across the sky, everywhere was bathed in a warm, pink glow as I looked down on the scene. Just imagine (I mused), Bach had been down there in 1720 and today, I was flying over at 500mph crossing border after border to play some of his music in the East. What would he have made of it all? Living then in such obscure circumstances, miles from anywhere and yet to many, he is the greatest composer of all time. Destiny, fame, fortune all came to mind as I turned, looking ahead into the oncoming darkness and the rose-pink aspect faded from view as we thundered onwards towards the Soviet Union.

On a later trip to the new Russian Federation I accepted an invitation to play in the north of Russia. Our itinerary took in the ancient Monastery of St. Kirill, the man who set down the old Russian script. He had lived in this amazing fortress of huge dimensions; the walls were 100ft thick. There, he slept in a house WITHOUT windows in temperatures below −30 Centigrade....he said that God would keep him warm and apparently, he survived this regime....and that is Faith.

Our own abode was a superb Dacha (wooden house) in a vast forest, which seemed to be larger than any English county. President Yeltsin had once stayed there and the whole area was fenced and patrolled by the Russian Army. On the night of the final concert, I took a taxi back with Nikolai and our cab jolted and bumped off the main highway and into the deep forest with snow-banks over a metre high on either side. A pale moon shone through the trees as we went down unfamiliar lanes; actually, the driver was lost. We turned a corner and saw an inky pool covering most of the road. Such areas can be very dangerous due to potholes of incredible depth and the driver revved hard and hurled the car forwards. My side of the car dipped into the pool and we almost slid into the blackness as waves splashed up the windows and over the bonnet; the driver laughed as the wipers zipped away and we only just made landfall and avoided a potential drowning.

Eventually our taxi found the way and after halting at the Guardroom, we were sent in and dropped right at our door. Once inside, I had a mind to open a beer....a good idea except we had left the opener at another dacha some 200 yards away. Undaunted, I walked out into the frost, sub-zero in North Russia, darkness for hundreds of miles, bright, odd stars above....a wild land with wolves, bears and even tigers. I mused on as the ice crunched under my feet and then, horror of horrors; SOMETHING was walking behind me!!! I stopped and the sound behind stopped too; I started off and the noise followed me....man OR BEAST? There was no option really and I had to turn to face whatever was stalking me, there was no cover to hand and no weaponry and running away could have been dangerous too. I turned and saw a huge dog, the same dog the Colonel had shown us on the first day, almost 5ft from nose to hind-legs. The dog halted and blinked and panted....I risked going on to the next dacha as the dog nuzzled my hand. The door was still open and I rushed in as the dog pushed hard to gain entry and then put its big paws up on the window reaching several feet up.

KIRILL MONASTERY-FORT, NORTH RUSSIA.
A section of the 100ft thick walls shows why no-one ever took this vast fortress. The small window is higher than a human, this being only part of the front wall; the gates are huge! This stands in the middle of nowhere. Neil Smith, collection.

NORTH RUSSIA, APRIL SNOW.
Here is the Colonel's dog about to investigate my guitar case. Our Dacha is at the right of picture, ahead is a lake over 200km long. Hardly noticed on maps in this enormous territory. Neil Smith, collection.

I at least had the opener but, how could I return safely? I saw a biscuit-box and took a handful out, opened the door slightly and gave a present to the hound. This idea worked and I emerged, dropping biscuits until I reached our dacha. The dog later sat on the verandah, watching me drink the beer. Next day I mentioned the incident and it seemed that I had been lucky. The dog had seen me on arrival the first day and knew me as a true guest: if I had NOT been a guest then I would have ended up in hospital or worse. This was a violent, military guard-dog, enough to put off even a heavy-criminal and I noticed later that its paws were actually as large as my hands. Good advice then not to go walking at night in the depths of an unknown forest in temperatures cold enough to make hot coffee cold in a matter of minutes, cold enough to freeze a canned-drink to your skin and to rip your skin away from the bone....dark and eerie enough to scare you to death when those sinister, stalking sounds haunt your every step.

And of course, Russia is a very, very large country indeed, many times larger than the United Kingdom. And as I went farther north, the world changed around me. Cold became the dominant feature everywhere and it was impossible to escape from this problem. As we journeyed along a small road into a massive (bigger than Yorkshire) forest, the bus in front suddenly lurched to the right and slid down a ravine: we halted and jumped out into the freezing cold ready to help. After a minute or two, people started to appear as they struggled up the slope....the bus had fortunately caught on some trees. They crammed onto our bus but not all could fit on and so they set out to walk onwards to our destination. Vodka was supplied to one and all and they also swigged from flasks as we set off; the bus would return later on, eventually, whenever. I stood at the crossroads in the middle of nowhere when our bus finally halted and could only see a large wooden house opposite which turned out to be a cafe/bar/meeting place/ whatever and we went in. As I sat down, a friend pointed to a sign on the wall....he translated:

ALL GUNS MUST BE LEFT HERE, BY ORDER!

This was to avoid a killing when tempers grew high and two hunting rifles and some handguns were hanging there menacingly. After dinner, we went outside to go further north, beyond into a rather virgin area of forest....so silent, it was eerie and we went on and on. Much later I found out that we were lost, not an uncommon thing in Russia and we all got out of the bus. A vodka flask was pushed into my gloves and I drank and felt a surge of warmth shooting through me as a man in eskimo-style garb approached us. The interpreter asked him about food, shelter, directions and he pointed to a wooden shack....I asked if he had a phone or radio or something and everyone laughed; this man had never had electricity in his whole life! And when I asked if I could write a letter to him or send a photo back to him the answer was no, his was not an address on a map; he killed deer for food and drank deer-blood if things got bad for him and his wife. The guide pointed at me and told the hunter I was from England....the hunter smiled and shook his head; he had never even heard of England! The guide asked me to speak a greeting in English and both the hunter and his wife blinked and opened their eyes wide, never had any foreign person spoken to them, ever. Amazing to meet people like this in the year 1997!

Darkness began to close in very quickly and the cold increased by leaps and bounds as the huge birch trees began to sparkle, almost as if a million pink candles had been lit by the last rays of the sun....I will never forget that sight. All at once, we heard a car engine whine from deep in the forest and we waited until the headlights shone through the mist. They say Russia is the ultimate land of contrasts and this day proved that fact to me. There in the middle of nowhere, a white Ford Sierra car with snowchains and a Russian plate drew up. The driver seemed to know the region and soon we piled back onto the bus, cursing because someone had left the doors open; everyone seemed pleased that this 'English car' had emerged from the gloom but I couldn't help puzzling about it all. An English car, so far north, no fuel, no service, no parts, nothing at all for backup....what was it all about? Does this not seem bizarre even now when told in a book? I took some photos of all this but sadly, they did not turn out....perhaps the cold had ruined the mechanism due to standing out for a while. I think back now; about that man and his wife, probably still hunting around there most likely. They both stacked a giant heap of logs against their back door for a REAL winter; I heard minus sixty degrees said once or twice. During that hellish time, they never go out, simply open the back door for more logs, smoke in the room for months, chewing on deer meat, drinking snow or blood. Makes going to the local shop seem a doddle actually.

Bonnie Scotland....the Forth Bridge, the Tay Bridge, the glens, lochs and the mountain mist. Many times these sights have met my eyes and I would agree with anyone who says that Scotland must be one of the most incredible places on the planet. Take The Clansman north by rail and you see some of the most fantastic scenery, meet an amazing array of people and drink the liquor that no-one can imitate.

One journey took me to Glasgow to stay over New Year and I left my guitar in the room for a time and strolled downstairs to see my friends in the main bar. This was not a night for serious 'guitar-work' and so I abandoned all ideas of sober study and decided to join in with whatever took place. We drank and drank....pints of 'heavy' and then a whisky now and then. After a few hours of this, the room seemed much brighter, much noisier and much happier than ever before as we caroused into the night. I took my leave of the party for a breath of fresh air and, as I did so, I heard loud music coming from a banquet room down the corridor. I could hear shouting and laughter along with the wild, highland music....pipes and drums for sure and not a recording but actually 'live' in the hotel. Time to go and see (I thought) and so I went along towards the growing din.

A party, with most people in highland dress and dancing up and down the room to a small ensemble. I had my bow-tie in my pocket and, since everything seemed quite formal I reclipped this around my neck and pushed my way to the dance floor. Certainly this was the place to be. People were clapping as men danced around the swords placed on the wooden boards; music, drink, dancing, food and many beautiful women too. I walked past the dancers and over to a table groaning with food and a man pushed a plate into my hand and pointed to the Angus beef and all trimmings; at the end of the table, a nice lady filled a wine glass and gave it to me. I took up a huge plateful and stood by eating as more noise and laughter shook the room; THIS was the place to be!

Soon, a charming lady came over to me and asked if I would dance. I may play music but I am NOT a dancer....she insisted that I should join in and so, I did. We danced for hours, or so it seemed and we danced up and down and in between raised arms and then, when our hands parted, she asked....

"I don't know you....which office are you from???"
I told her that I was from the Manchester branch and, as we twirled away from each other she shouted out....

"We don't have a Manchester office!"
I simply carried on jumping around, not noticing some large, kilted men approaching through the throng....towards ME! Fortunately, everyone was so drunk that they proved unable to detect my accent and they patted me on the shoulder as I staggered out into the night.

I played at Appleby Castle on several occasions (by the way, the House That Jack Built is actually in the town) and stayed with wonderful friends there, Dr and Mrs Cooper who were always so kind to me. My next concert on one winter trip was at York and I had foolishly left my petrol tank on low: never do this in deep winter out in the wilds. We took petrol from an ancient car in the garage and had to filter it as we sent it thru to the tank of my car. The wind howled like a real gale and snow began to fall....deep, REALLY deep. My journey took the A66 road across Stainmore which can be rather pretty in summer but in a severe winter, the whole event can be quite scary....especially if you have no petrol: red light on almost all of the journey. At every dip in the road, I took my foot off the pedal and often just drifted along: there was no other way and the snow banks began to mount up at either side of me, the distant ridges above the Lune Forest seemed quite menacing as I moved onwards, eyes glued to the dashboard.

Soon, I had reached a real high point in the road and the snow banks were truly enormous (above room height) and the red light stayed on without blinking! The cold was intense too and on the crest of a hill, I stopped the car and looked around....for as far as I could see, the huge walls of snow held me prisoner. Looking down the view ahead, I could see a light flashing, a blue light far, far away in the distance and so I drifted down towards the approximate position of the light on the <u>other</u> side of this barrier of snow. Stopping my car, I ventured out into hellish cold: this was truly Arctic weather and I was on a slim single-lane highway, flashing hazards and expecting a smash in the back at any moment. The snow walls towered above me: truly in Britain on normal roads, I have seen nothing like this! Trying to guess where the blue light had flashed, I climbed onto the top of my car and hauled myself onto the snow ridge between lanes. Once on top, I saw a police car to my right, maybe 50 yards away and I scrambled over. As I dropped down, the officer (reading a paper) turned to me....

"Bloody Hell! Where did you come from? No-one is on this road today! You'll die if you don't get inside and keep warm!"

I told him of my dilemma and he shook his head: the nearest petrol on Sunday was at Scotch Corner! He warned me seriously about my situation and said that I should abandon my car and stay in his car until duty finished late in the day. Knowing I had to play in York at 8pm, I declined his offer and set off back over the ridge: he shouted at me again, this time with a real scream and I halted on the ridge looking around at the incredible landscape. Yes, I had seen this kind of snowscene before in Norway very high up and yes, people did <u>DIE</u> in this type of cold, make no mistake. I shouted back to the officer that I was going to try my luck and he shook his head and shouted "Good Luck!"

Moving on, I expected the car to conk out at any moment, hardly touching the accelerator I went on and on and the snow walls reduced a little to my relief. Eventually, I went past some cottages and on and on until I saw the fuel station at Scotch Corner....almost as soon as I sighted the place, the car started coughing and spluttering and finally it gave out almost on the entrance drive to the depot! I asked a lorry driver to help me to push the car onto the forecourt, telling him of the adventure as I did so....he shook his head and was not amused. Well yes, he thought that I was a fool to risk my life to get across that terrain on that day and he told me so in the best 'Driver's English' one could imagine!

I went onwards to York, ice and snow en-route but nothing like the hazards I had been through up north. The concert was for York University Guitar Society in the wonderful setting of The King's Manor Cellar, the old wine store for the King in days gone by. The place still had a smell of long-ago beer and wine and I still recall the vaulted ceilings and the echo of my guitar as I played that night. Once more I decided to stay in the city and not to venture across the stark hills between....enough of this survival and SAS routine: I opted for clean sheets in a small hotel and saw the TV shots of the main motorways blocked solid with ice and snow as I settled down, safe and sound.

Danger of a different kind found me during a trip to France where, on a sizzling, baking hot day, we ran out of water and food: the heat was so intense that it was impossible to hold on to the steering wheel in our car. A village shimmered in the haze ahead and we drove in to find a sleepy hamlet, not a soul in sight, grass blowing in clumps across the dusty road: the place could have been used in a Western! We got out of the car and very slowly dragged our legs up the hill....only a rather grotty-looking dog ambled down towards us, its tongue hanging out and staring at us with wild eyes. It stopped as if to challenge us and then, wandered off into a back alley.

Further up the hill, we came across a boarded-up cafe with the tables and chairs piled outside: truly, no-one was to be seen, the whole village seemed dead, lifeless. A large blackboard stood in front of the cafe obviously used to write down menus, etc. Turning to look at the board, I was horror-stricken to see a crude skull-and-crossbones drawn in chalk and one deadly word below it....RABIES! I looked at John and we both spun round to see where the dog had vanished and began to walk quickly back to our car. Everyone was moaning and groaning when we returned until we told our story: the windows were rolled up, doors locked and we revved the engine to climb the hill and get out of town....Pronto! Several miles farther on we stopped at a civilised village and managed to extract from the reluctant inhabitants facts that confirmed our fears....there was an outbreak of the deadly plague, some dogs had been shot dead, others locked away and some residents had gone away for a while into safety. Still not wishing to make a long halt, we drove on away from this cursed place, forgetting our thirst until we came across a little bistro, a wonderful oasis in the setting sun where we ate and drank the night away with our guitars: a day best forgotten!

Travelling around so much on a regular basis could so easily turn into a chore, especially if taken to excess; once I was away for thirteen weeks out of fifteen <u>and</u> in seven different countries <u>and</u> all over the UK too. One can easily become blasé about dangerous situations or even be unaware of them.

I stayed in New York a few times and I was warned about the real danger of being out at night alone. Daytime problems did not seem apparent until they stared me in the face. As I left town one day, I crossed Broadway and went towards a small shop. A little (9 years?) boy asked me in a very polite manner to buy him a knife in the shop window and he held out a ten-dollar bill to pay for it. Fortunately, I ignored his request and once inside the counter-teller gave me a lecture....

"Did that kid ask you to buy a knife? (I nodded) He would stick it in your guts as soon as you gave it to him! You watch out boy!"

I thanked the guy for his advice as the young kid pulled faces at the window and shouted abuse through the shop door. I wandered off intending to walk up Harlem past the famous Apollo Theatre and nearby, I saw a flashy but 'heavy' guy standing in a dark doorway. He saw me coming and pointed to my guitar as he shouted out....

"*Hey music-man, come here. You need some stuff, right? We've got it all down here....you know, REAL stuff; know what I mean?*"

I told him that I never needed any 'stuff' and just as I spoke, a policeman (who had obviously been watching) slammed his car door hard, stared aggressively at both of us <u>and</u> put his hand on his revolver! Our trio seemed rather odd standing in the street and I figured it was a safe bet to walk over near the cop rather than stand close to my uninvited friend. The flash-guy just leered at us both, shook his head and made his way down into his underworld cavern: He would be back later, and the cops would not catch him next time.

I used the underpass one day to go to the garage and as I stepped out into the sun, I saw three police officers talking to a man in a pink (!) suit. The man issued the orders.....

"*Ok, now listen. You two follow me into the front and wait. You go up the fire escape and wait for anyone jumping out. Give me five minutes then we go. Check your watches...now check your guns.*"

So saying they all took out revolvers, broke open the guns and spun the chambers. The guns were closed and they walked off into the underpass as a passing pedestrian mumbled "Drugs-Bust!" As I saw them vanish on that bright, sunny day, I couldn't help but think about the lives of such lawmen. Here in broad daylight, a drama was unfolding which could have resulted in bullets, blood and death: How about that for a job? I got into the car feeling at least a little safer surrounded by sirens.

BROADWAY AND HARLEM MEET....
Off to retrace my journey to the famous Apollo Theatre as I leave the subway at 125th Street, New York, USA. No kids with knives this time!   Courtesy, Elaine Webb

People often ask about my guitars, particularly the so called Spanish (classical) Guitars. I have been fortunate to have two guitars made for me by leading makers, one already mentioned by Mass K. Hirade in Japan and also my favourite guitar, made by Martin Fleeson.

Martin was Australian by birth but he had emigrated to England where he lived in Nantwich, Cheshire for many years. I met him on a visit to play for Chester Guitar Society and he brought along a few guitars. It was evident from the way he spoke about the wood, the craftsmanship, the knowledge of sonority that he had some special quality there in his work. I took home no less than four guitars on loan that night and, though they were good, they did not beat my favourite guitar at the time, a Marcelino Lopez model which had apparently been tried out by the great Andres Segovia. I phoned Martin and, needless to say he was disappointed and so we agreed to meet at a junction on the M6 Motorway where he could collect his guitars as I drove down to Birmingham for a concert. When we met, I could see that he was not pleased and so he turned to me and said...

"I'll make you a guitar you won't forget!"

I shook his hand and told him to make it and I would play it.

Months later with my Wigmore debut approaching, I got a call from Martin and I went down with my wife to view some guitars. He had three or four made and he told me that each one took him about five weeks to make, the top-table wood he selected himself from a spruce tree he bought in Switzerland and as I played, our wives chatted and strolled around the house. I played one guitar and it felt just right and, as if to prove that, both women came back into the room and asked which guitar had just been playing. Without hesitation, I took this guitar and, months later, the press praised the sound when I sat on stage at the Wigmore 19th January 1979, the blackest day in the dark Winter of Discontent. Martin phoned later and sounded so pleased and soon his order books started to fill up as I took the guitar to dozens of countries around the globe.

Martin and myself were joint guests at the Cannington Course in the 1980's and he left a couple of guitars behind with me for students to try. En route home, my train stopped at Crewe Station and Martin was there, beaming from ear to ear. As I gave him back one guitar he burst out.....

"You'll never guess; John Williams has ordered two of my guitars!"

This special event had come about partly due to our joint belief in his guitars and I felt so pleased for him that day. His guitars took a leap forward on the world-stage and everywhere, players asked about this special, clear, loud guitar....a walking advert. Sadly, the story ends soon. Later on holiday, Martin was taken ill and within a few weeks, had passed away. When you look at record labels of John Williams, myself and others, think when you see that name Fleeson. A great talent. A natural really who took guitar making forward into the new age of concert guitar and still had great visions for the future.

The Eighties represent, still today, a time of almost excessive spending, a time where 'image' counted more than at any other time and (at least, to me) a time when social-caring seemed to increase and yet real compassion evaporated. I have written elsewhere in the volume of the artistic struggle to survive and in this brief encounter, we will see how it is possible to get ahead, to worm one's way forward even if one has little or no talent. Some may be shocked by what I set down now, others who know the business will simply smile and nod.

In 1980, I was asked to sample some Japanese guitars made by Mass K. Hirade, a maker second only to Masaru Kohno, the great guitar maker from Tokyo. Mr Hirade arrived with his entourage at the hotel; lawyers, advisors, specialists and another man who seemed connected to publicity. I played one of Hirade's guitars and he was so impressed that he offered to make me a "Super-Model" for my use only (he did actually do this and gave it to me as a gift in 1981). As lunch progressed, I met the publicity guy and found out that he had himself worked for one of the former British prime ministers. We talked of business; the music business and my new friend did admit that he knew absolutely nothing about the music side of things... BUT he did know how to present and promote people, things, events. In short, it did not matter to him whether a product OR person was good or bad...he saw his sole job as finding a way to promote it to the world.

As we talked on and on, he picked up a large Cuban cigar and lit it and eyed me through the smoke as he did so. His questions came thick and fast. How much money did I make? How much capital did I have? Could I get some financial backing? Could I invest at least a third of my income per year on publicity <u>alone</u>? I answered as well as I could, at times he nodded with approval, sometimes he just sucked in his breath and shook his head. Already I was moving into a bigger financial area than expected, an area which at that time, was open only to the wealthy few OR to those people, with or without talent able to obtain enough dollars. The conversation in the whole place was humming, guitar music was playing on a disc in the background and my new friend asked if the playing was my own...it was not. Suddenly, out of the blue, he asked me a rather surprising question...

"*How famous do you <u>want</u> to be Neil?*"

I stopped speaking and thought: Fame, fortune, travel, riches all on an international scale. Who would not wish for that? And so I told him my hopes and plans as he nodded away, smiling as the smoke drifted around us. Bear in mind that this man had helped politicians and massive companies to achieve their goals, he said...

"*My advice would normally be <u>very</u> expensive but I can say to you Neil that for £100,000, our company could make you the most famous player currently active in the world!*"

For that money (in 1980) he knew that he could make ANYBODY famous and I was assured later that he really did have all the right connections too. So there it was...Fame could be bought...as simple as that! The next time you see a new face on tv, especially a face turning up regularly on show after show, in magazine upon magazine, always in prime-time without any prior notice (publicly) of their coming to fame then, ask yourself the question. And ask even more questions if that person or band has little or no ability in their chosen field. Perhaps it seems cynical to say such things and yet, if this is the Truth, then let it be known. That figure of £100,000 would not of course apply today; mark that up by a large amount and doors will open for you NOW, whatever your subject. Disturbing? Surely it is, and what a sad comment on the entertainment industry in particular for those who are presently honestly struggling to make it big...not to mention the political implications of all of this. Perhaps even sadder is the fact that I am writing this knowing that I did not have one hundred thousand pounds to spare at the time!

My father would not have been amused nor surprised by all of this; he always said that there was a rather strange side to show business in his opinion. Already in this volume I have mentioned odd characters and guns too. When I described these events to my father and added a detailed account of the gun (an American Service Automatic pistol) he was horrified...rightly so since I was just over sixteen years old. Eventually, I came across crooks of another kind; if you are about to sign a contract, read on before you do so.

In 1969 as a struggling player, I penned some small tunes down one day on my guitar and set them at one side in a drawer. Ten years on I was working at a studio on sessions and the studio boss asked me if I had any material for a compilation album. Next day, my pieces were recorded and I signed a royalty deal which gave me 50% ownership of the works in return for the studio promoting them on our 'mutual behalf' ...it sounded ok at the time but, wait and see. Several years later I was touring Scandinavia and as I prepared for the evening concert, I happened to play an extract from one of my small pieces; everyone in the house came into the room asking me about the music....it was on national tv most days, every week!!!! The recording studio had obviously sold the rights and given me nothing, not a penny! I checked around and it was true; my music and MY recording playing as a travel service and weather jingle! I returned to the UK angry and determined.

By my rough calculations, I had lost 50% of anything up to £55,000 and maybe more if the service went across national borders. My solicitor had advice for me but my first port of call had to be the studio since I had a legal right to see any accounts on demand. Knowing what the studio could be like in disputes (violence had erupted twice there) I took along Mike, an ex-detective friend who stood a humbling 2 metres tall...he was instructed to listen closely to any conversations and if necessary, to act against anyone moving against me. Mike could be very, very unfriendly if the occasion warranted this mode of action. As so often happens, the studio was in the process of a refit and no access to documents seemed possible. The studio boss eyed my new friend with great suspicion, never even speaking to Mike but always watching him as our conversation dawdled on and on. I made my point eventually and a frosty attitude came over the meeting...the boss agreed to see what he could do (in other words, to cover his tracks up) and curtly ended the talks, never once did he speak to Mike.

Months later, I went to London to play at the Purcell Room and to give a few small concerts around town. One night, I stayed at a sumptuous house, a mansion really and I was told that it belonged to a QC...a Queen's Counsel no less. He arrived late for dinner and we chatted over this and that subject, my new friend seemed to know something about everything in the world including music. He had worked on libel cases but, more interesting for me, on copyright law cases and so I broached the subject directly and told him of the raw deal I had stumbled upon. Yes, it was obvious that I was entitled to money because the music was mine and the performance was mine also. The trouble was that any company would wait and see and even risk going to The Courts in an attempt to stave off paying out directly to a client. In effect, I learned that copyright means nothing if one does not have the money-muscle to back up a claim. Anything can be stolen, used, made, copied until someone issues a legal challenge to stop the offender. To issue that challenge would be costly in the UK Courts...exactly how much was totted up by my colleague

"Well let's see...I would need say £77,000 to start your case off and beyond that, if another case is anything to go by, you could be looking at another £90,000. Let's say £177,000 all in to be sure. Then of course, we have to win or you could be liable for their costs too!"

We agreed that half of my expected royalties did not warrant such a risk and so the bad guys won without firing a shot. Much later, they went bankrupt.

Without becoming too caustic about the whole of the entertainment scene, I can give here and now a few examples of why any particular 'name' may or may not make it big. Again, these events are absolutely true and someone, somewhere should be embarrassed that they are deeply implicated in such dealings.

When I began to work internationally, I made every effort to improve my repertoire especially works with orchestra since these pieces are rewarding musically and financially. One day I arrived home around midday and my wife told me excitedly that a big-time agent was phoning back at around 4pm. Impatiently I waited and at exactly four, the phone rang and the agent asked if I was free to play the famous Rodrigo Concerto on a certain date; I was free. Having cleared that hurdle, the agent spoke of a large fee...but there was a catch. I was to deputize for (..........) an EXTREMELY famous player and a condition of the deal was that I could never mention this player's name on publicity! I was a young player taking over for a truly great artist and it would never be known to the public and so I would not gain kudos from this event. The reader may find this so puzzling; read on for more of the same.

One of my friends knew a good female singer, a really superb professional vocalist. Out of the blue, she was offered a wonderful European tour, tv appearances and top hotels...everything. She was overjoyed but, there was a catch: the bottom line was that she had to live-in with the tour manager. No live-in, no tour. Her name has never been in the Charts but, are you surprised really? Once, my own name was my downfall! A recording exec asked around for a new, quality guitarist and (nothing to do with me) my name was given to him no less than three times by experts. Eventually I found out that I had lost the world-wide record deal; the recordings were of Spanish music and my name did not have the right 'ring' to it....that was all. Snookered by my own name! On another occasion a high-up artsperson asked me to play at his home privately for a bash; no money, no expenses offered at all. I already had another booking that night but, you guessed right, it was held against me by that person. He avoided me from then on and my agents and for all I know, could even have deliberately stood in the way of my career. And that is it, no-one will ever know the truth because unlike a routine/regular job, these things cannot be monitored by anyone, not supervised, clarified nor even held to account by a legal piece of paper as we have already noted. Don't put your daughter on the stage, Mrs Worthington, Don't put your daughter on the stage.

Any player who survives all of this flak and gains recognition around the globe is indeed charmed. Originally I had thought that this kind of backstabbing and crawling was confined to the Pop business since it is well known that connections are incredibly important in that field but of course, there is no reason to imagine that it is confined to any single area or event. Big money is involved in a mega record or tour deal and where there is money to be made and spent, then there you can find all manner of behind the scene activity; I well recall a quite poor band taking the stage before our group. They were terrible and it emerged later that the lady promoter of the evening was actually the mother of two of the 'Guests' on our show. Still, they played for free and we got away with a relatively short night so maybe no harm was done all round. Looking at it another way, would the reader like someone to enter his/her working environment and simply take over one's job for no pay: <u>for free</u>? No need to reply; I know the answer already.

As another gloomy winter approached, I noted an unusual period of congestion in my diary; four or five events in one week, each with a different orchestra...playing a different concerto each night! Perhaps only a player can convey the significance of such a complex situation; rather like a chess-player dealing with a few games at the same moment. The phone rang and it was Helen Jennings, my London agent at the time, offering me a date at the new St. David's Hall, Cardiff ...a concerto date again and in the same week as the rest. I agreed to do the job, thinking that I would simply have to use one of the items already on tour. No such luck! Back came a contract asking for two items new to me: Giuliani's Guitar Concerto and Malcolm Arnold's Serenade. This request upped the workload considerably since few <u>string</u> players would eagerly take on seven different concertos in six days with a travel span from Scotland to the South West of England and into Wales. Additionally, news came in that one of the nights could involve a 'Direct-Broadcast' on radio...a whole parcel of extra rehearsal and hassle. I rechecked about the Cardiff items; surely it did not <u>have</u> to be these two beautiful (but little-played) works. The conductor was the noted writer and broadcaster Antony Hopkins and he specifically asked for these pieces in advance, the whole programme was revolving around such pieces. As the week loomed ahead, I took time out to study like a crazy-man the reams and reams of paper lying about the room. I recall kicking the tour off, moving through ice, rain and snow, taking three white shirts and washing in some hotel rooms, laundering in other places and always, that next gig, staring me in the face. And it all came together on each night...as I walked off after the final event, I saw myself in the stageside mirror. Yes, I was tired, <u>very</u> tired and I decided to stay overnight rather than risk one of my famous 'Night-Rides' ... with the prospect of crashing through tiredness or perhaps meeting yet another wild man on the road.

Small wonder then that some people turn to drink or drugs in order to 'keep their head on'...or is it to lose it? Ideally, one should be carried away by the music, not something else. The guitar itself presents enough problems for one lifetime, becoming 'spaced-out' can only add to it all and some styles of music suffer more than most if the player is not 100% in charge. To the general public, one guitar is like another but all players know that there are specific dividing lines and it is hard to find a player who is truly a master of ALL styles. Listening around the world, one can hear an incredible variety of guitar music and to master one style would take many years, even if such mastery is possible. Many would say (and I agree) that the guitar has universal appeal and when guitar-players meet, it seems to matter less what style is played, the guitar forms an instant bond. Nero did not 'fiddle' when Rome burned...he was a guitarist!

For a time, I too became involved in the cult of the 'First Performance' where a player (or players) play in public a new composition and this attracts attention to the new piece and also to those who perform it. This side of 'career-development' is much nicer than simply edging the way ahead...or creeping, as my father termed it. And even a third-performance can attract attention as happened when I played The Blue Guitar by Sir Michael Tippett on the occasion of his birthday. I also met Peter Racine-Fricker when he was President of Cheltenham Festival and played his piece Paseo there. The great Ukrainian composer Stepan Rak once wrote a piece 'on the lunch-table' ...straight from his head, no instrument at all as we ate all around him <u>and</u> that night, we played it in concert. I guess that this is truly what is known as Tafelmusik, what else? Once, our duo did an evening of several premieres and four composers arrived to listen-in. I noted that one man looked distinctly solemn, almost a recluse wearing a old-fashioned mackintosh and scruffy shoes. When his piece had ended, the audience applauded modestly and he suddenly jumped up, opened his mac and produced a small Union Jack Flag on a stick and he proceeded to wave this around with great abandon until the less-than-furious applause subsided. You can't beat enthusiasm; especially for your own music! The opposite of this scenario came when I played at a large club near Leeds as a deputy for a country-band. As we arrived at sundown, we unloaded the van with our jeans, boots, cowboy-shirts and all draped over our shoulders. A rather odd, goofy-looking man approached from the club doorway and said..

"They don't like Country-Music here!"
I won't bother printing my reply.

Some of the times described here are tinged for me with a mixture of sadness and happiness. My second divorce loomed ahead and the ending of that marriage was truly disturbing and even violent; if the reader has been through a 'regular' divorce then the feelings can be multiplied ten times in such circumstances as mine. My guitar provided me with wonderful escape-routes to sanity, sometimes whisking me away within hours of dealing with the most disturbing scenes at home and I boarded various jets with a pioneering outlook, leaving all my cares behind me.

In that deep winter, I had a call from Karen Gerrard, a good friend and great entrepreneur who wanted me to co-direct a guitar course in Spain with my old friend Simon Dinnigan. The course was at Lliber (pronounced Yeeber) in the Jalon Valley, Costa Brava. Somewhat opposite Ibiza, a beautiful valley filled with orange groves and tiny villages. We set off from Gatwick in a howling rainstorm and, on board the jet, I noticed the tv-show hosts, Richard and Judy as I swung the guitar into the overhead locker. Richard looked up and looked puzzled and said...

"Excuse me but don't I know you from somewhere?"
I nodded and told him about the morning show I had played on from the Liverpool Docks. They were off to a villa also in the same region as our party, an area favoured by the British and ex-patriots. Our villa had many rooms and a pool and one day, on a course-break, Simon and I set off into the mountains. Once there, our tiny car began driving through piles of oranges that had blown down in a storm. Rather than waste these, we collected some off the road (NOT the trees or paths) and the car was filled

PROMS CONCERT WITH ROBERT HARDY.
This great actor narrated speeches of Winston Churchill to the music of Walton at Belvoir Castle and Castle Howard....really large events, one of them for some 18,000 people outdoors.   Neil Smith, collection.

PROMS CONCERT WITH GEORGE MELLY.
I told him the best joke he had heard all year....he said that I should have been a comedian. Maybe I am one!   Neil Smith, collection.

with that incredible scent of orange juice as we wound our way back into the sunset. A day later it was Christmas and we bought masses of tomatoes, fruit, bread and champagne and could see the fireworks going off over the hills in Alicante and at midnight, I somehow fell into the swimming pool fully-clothed. I still don't know how it happened, honestly.

One of the things about such events is that the courses are self-catering and it falls to everyone to provide meal-deals or ideas. Mine was simple but effective and I can describe it now for all to try. Buy dozens of tomatoes and fresh bread and lean, <u>micro</u>-thin bacon; as thin as a five-pence coin and NO thicker. Chop the tomatoes and bacon into small pieces, put in a deep pan and heat slowly until the mixture is not only hot but has rather a paste-like constituency. Add Worcester Sauce or a little puree to taste, salt and pepper too. Butter the bread thick and get a glass of cheap white wine to go with it and serve the hot dish in a soup bowl, dipping bread in as you go. Nothing quite like this on a sunny morning sat by the pool; make plenty because people always seem to want more, especially if the chef has got the right touch and long experience like Chef Smith and his happy band. Desayuno de la Guitarra.

It was with the greatest reluctance that we boarded the plane back to Blighty and at times, we 'helped' each other to negotiate the aisles or steps and our noisy arrival at Gatwick did not amuse everyone I seem to remember. Once outside, the icy wind and rain threw me down mentally; don't get me wrong. England is a great place but our weather can be so depressing and you know it is the end of a trip when you feel the cold air and can only glance back at your good times.

As I write this final chapter, I recall some of my recent trips; to Arabia, to Japan and once more, to Russia. A fax has just come in from New York about a trip and a letter from Brazil and my latest CD will be issued two weeks from today. Not only this. On August 5th, 2000, I was chosen to play at Glamis Castle, Scotland, the home of Her Royal Highness, The Queen Mother for her birthday celebrations; almost 6,000 people turned up for the night...a night to remember. And I would like all of my future concerts to be memorable like the time I played next to the Viking Longships or that special day at London's Barbican or that eerie experience playing at Attila's Hall of The Mountain King. In recent times, I have taken to a few big Proms-style events, outdoor with vast audiences and famous names; the actor Robert Hardy, singers like Sarah Walker and George Melly and the actor/compere Tony (Baldrick) Robinson. These days, I tend to keep more photos than before and some can be found in this volume. The Roar of the Greasepaint, the Smell of the Crowd...even though my main work is classical, I guess that this is what my work is about.

Looking through a photo album for this book the other day, I came across my very first school photo and suddenly, I saw the school as it used to be and my pals too; Graham, Dorothy, Colin, Brian and the rest and it all made me wonder...what happened to everyone? Certainly, we all grow and go onwards towards Fate, Destiny, Life. Never in my wildest dreams did I think that I would see 'actual' Red Indians and cowboys too, or that I would fly the Rockies or down the Grand Canyon, Death Valley, see the Pacific Ocean, the Atlantic, the Mongolian Desert, the vast Steppes in the East, the fjords of Norway, the Arabian sunrise and more all due to my music, <u>not</u> on holiday, paying for every mile. Music opens so many doors for people, almost without limits; the bustle and speed of New York, night-life in Paris, the grandeur of Rome or Athens, the heat and style of Hollywood, the Unter den Linden in Berlin, the mighty Kremlin in Moscow, Niagra Falls, Alicante or the Northern Lights in Scotland as I stood on the battlefield of Culloden. So many places to see...too many for one lifetime I guess.

And the events bring people to mind; the Good, the Bad and the Ugly. They all have invaded my life. Santino with his guitar on a wild spree in Rome, rich and famous persons too and the brave men like Tassos and Vlad whose tales would have a listener rivetted to a seat. And those difficult officials, some of whom pointed LOADED guns at me and not forgetting that wintry night long ago when that killer failed to finish me off. My impressions are strong and can be recalled in a moment as I drive in my head down the baking Autostrada past Florence or stand in the mist at the Brandenburg Gate, looking across that sinister Wall, drive past Olympus or walk through Pompeii, stand before the grave of Edvard Grieg the composer or play a candle-lit concert in the palace of a duke in a remote part of Italy. These things have happened to me for a reason ...I'm not sure what the reason is yet but, much of it has been fun.

Some of these things do seem to me to be like rather difficult 'Tests' in the already complex life I lead: a life which includes two divorces, the tragic suicide of my mother and the tragic deaths of my own son and one grand'daughter....things that I know could (and have) put some people away for a long time in care, let alone survive it all AND carry on with an international career. HAVE GUITAR, WILL TRAVEL has maybe given an insight into my world of success, failure, fun and danger. It did all happen as I describe here and maybe the reader will find some of the events truly unforgettable. The world behind the stage can be a remote and lonely place at times and few people can step back there in order to see exactly what goes on: being honest, most jobs seem boring by comparison. Some may say that it is a Life of Riley (as they say up North). Surely there can be an element of this but, recall that I have been on both sides; hands and face covered in oil, fingers bleeding, back bent with heavy loads and (more than once) I have almost died as high-voltages sparked and surged near my hands. Music is not so dangerous but it does require skill, dedication and courage to get out there... try it yourself if you don't believe me! It also requires an incredible amount of work and this is not always appreciated as my final quote will show. My friend Geoffrey Walls was a singer on radio post-war and he was leaving the studios one night when a city-gent came over to ask for his autograph. The man opened up with...

"Oh Mr Walls! I must say how much I enjoyed your singing. I have seen you so often here and there...do tell me; how do you manage to get time off work?"

Geoffrey concluded the story....

"Neil, I simply turned away, threw my scarf around my neck and strode off into the night!"

GLAMIS CASTLE, SCOTLAND, August 5, 2000.
Waiting to rehearse the Rodrigo Concerto for the 100th Birthday of HRH The Queen Mother. Outdoor concert and the audience are arriving already for a big night out....5,800 people at least.   Neil Smith, collection.

TROLDHAUGEN, HOME OF EDVARD GRIEG, NORWEGIAN COMPOSER.
Here in an amazing setting worked Grieg, alone by a frozen lake. He was buried with his wife in a mountain face near the lake. This is January 1980, sub-zero and at night, my fingers almost froze before the concert.
Courtesy, Torsten Lind.

NEIL SMITH PUBLICATIONS, RECORDINGS, ETC, ETC........
Monthly contributor to Classical Guitar, the international magazine for classical guitarists. Also Music Editor for same.
Email: classicalguitar@ashleymark.co.uk

RECORDINGS TO DATE.........
Year/Issue   1981 PENNINE RECORDS, LP title,CLASSICALGUITAR (deleted)
1984 GUITAR MASTERS, LP title, GUITAR MUSIC OF JOHN W DUARTE
1990 XLCR RECORDINGS, Cassette title, VIRTUOSO (sold out)
1994 APOYO RECORDS, CD title, LA DANZA
2000 FORSYTHS, CD w/Recorder/Voice title, HERE WE COME A -PIPING
2000 HLM CLASSICS, CD title, VISTA DEL SUR

BOOKS AND MUSIC............
SIX DANCES by Michael Praetorius. Settings of favourite dances from Terpsichore, 1612, edited by Neil Smith. Published Lathkill Music www.lathkillmusic.co.uk
HAVE GUITAR, WILL TRAVEL. Travel tales from Neil Smith in a short book. Available from Laithkill Music (above) or direct from the author below.

COURSES, etc, etc.
Annual guitar courses in Scotland with many other international players.
Details from Email: oatridgeinternational@scotguitar.demon.co.uk
Occasional courses for West Dean College, Chichester, UK.

NEIL SMITH AGENTS.........
BRITAIN .....ARENA ENTERTAINMENTS
0113 239 2222 (Call Martin Nazaruk)
Email: stars@arenaentertainments.co.uk
WORLD...HLM GUITAR AGENCY, HOLLAND
0031 26 3615444
(Call Sjoerd van der Meulen)
Email: hlmhouse@globalxs.nl

AUTHOR'S DETAILS.........
WEBSITE........www.guitaristuk.com
Email........neilsmithguitar@amserve.net
Mobile........ 07818431575

Neil Smith uses D'ADDARIO Guitar Strings, made in the USA.